"Schroeder has written a wickedly funny yet meaningful memoir, a page-turner that the late Erma Bombeck might have penned had she served in the House of Representatives."

—Grace Lichtenstein, *The Washington Post*

"Patricia Schroeder has written a terrific memoir of her years in the House. Smart, funny, and candid, as she is, it is a trip through contemporary politics and family life, feminist style."

—Judy Mann, *The Washington Post*

"This book on how the Congress really works would be frightening if Schroeder's black humor didn't have you laughing so hard."

—*Publishers Weekly*

"This book is loaded with tantalizing tidbits."

—*Boston Globe*

"Written with warmth, vivacity, and humor, this is also the story of how one woman balanced her public and private lives."

—*Rossmoor News*

24 Years of House Work . . .
and the Place Is Still a Mess

My Life in Politics

Pat Schroeder

**Andrews McMeel
Publishing**

Kansas City

www.andrewsmcmeel.com

99 00 01 02 03   RDH   10 9 8 7 6 5 4 3 2 1

A hardcover edition of this book was published in 1998 by Andrews McMeel Publishing.

Library of Congress Cataloging in Publication Data
As Cataologued for the Hardcover Version
Schroeder, Pat.
    24 years of House work—and the place is still a mess : my life in politics / Pat Schroeder.
        p.   cm.
    ISBN 0-8362-8734-7
    1. Schroeder, Pat 2. Women legislators—United States—Biography. 3. Legislators—United States—Biography. 4. United States. Congress. Senate—Biography. 5. United States—Politics and government—1945–1989. 6. United States—Politics and government—1989– I. Title.
E840.8.S36A3   1998
328.73'092—dc21   98–12336
    [B]   CIP

Contents

Preface

A few words about this book:

If you want dirt, buy a tabloid.

If you want a string of bill numbers and wonkish policy memos, get the *Congressional Record*.

This book is about how it felt to be inside the "whale"—Congress during the last quarter-century. This is my recollection of what it was like entering that forbidding place with a young, spirited family and a driving desire to make a difference.

I felt swallowed by Congress: Every day was a fight to survive and not sell out. But I know that millions of women all over this country had similar experiences as we went through the cataclysmic changes required for doors to open to women.

This book is as true and as honest as I can make it.

Pat Schroeder

Acknowledgments

There is no twelve-step program for recovering politicians, but perhaps there should be. For twenty-four years, everything I wanted to say in Congress had to be shoe-horned into one minute, five minutes, whatever time I could persuade the esteemed gentleman from Massachusetts or Texas or Georgia to yield to me. Such frustration! So much to say and so little time! I'm grateful to have this chance to complete some thoughts about being one of the few women serving in Congress. This is step one to recovery!

So many people have extended their help and friendship during my political career. I really want to thank those progressive, forward-thinking voters in Denver who took a chance and voted for me in 1972. They launched me, and I'm eternally grateful.

Megathanks to the friends and staff who navigated the

political seas with me over the last twenty-four years. They're the best friends and constituents anyone could have asked for.

Thanks, too, to Mel Berger, Aimee Lee Ball, Chris Schillig and especially the big kahuna, Jake Morrissey, for thinking that I had something to say and letting me say it—my way!

Finally, I've been blessed with the world's best husband, kids and family. They're the reason I'm still standing; they're the reason I still care so much.

Schroeder's 24 Years of House Work and Achievements

Number of Political Consultants Hired: 0

Average Election-Winning Percentage: 62%

Number of Polls Taken: 0

Average Campaign Contribution
   from Individuals: $32.96

Number of Newsletters Mailed: 1

Number of Letters Received: 1,700,000

Number of Letters Returned: 1,699,999

Number of Phone Calls Received: 350,000

Number of Hours Working for Constituents: 78,000

Number of Days Spent Working in Washington: 3,000

Number of Constituent Problems Handled: 100,000

Number of Indictments: 0

Number of Media Interviews: 10,000 and counting

Number of Husbands: 1

Number of Bean Burritos Eaten in Office: 4,500

Number of Regrets: 0

1

Kamikaze Run

As I drove away from Capitol Hill for the last time as a member of Congress, I caught a glimpse in the rearview mirror of the Capitol dome, that symbol of so much hope and promise, so much cynicism and disappointment. It was then that I realized my House work was done. After twenty-four years, it wasn't finished—housework never is—but mine was over. Nearly a quarter of a century in a federal institution is enough.

I remembered someone had told me that the dome had been built at the height of the Civil War and that many people considered it the ultimate folly—who builds something like that during wartime? But Abraham Lincoln approved: The new dome could be seen from across the Potomac in Virginia—the Confederacy—and he understood it was a symbol that the Union would prevail.

Lots of people thought my decision to enter politics a little more than a hundred years after that would prove to be *my* folly. Friends often asked why I would engage myself so publicly, put myself in the way of so much antagonism, humiliation and second-guessing by those who thought differently on the issues. I was never a shrinking violet, but I don't think I would ever have exposed myself to the travails of political life if I hadn't been given last rites at age thirty, almost bleeding to death after giving birth to my daughter. That little ceremony gets your attention!

I'm sure my willingness to stick my neck out and take some big risks comes from learning so young not to take life for granted. I'm driven to sample everything I can as fast as possible.

My husband, Jim, didn't want me to leave the House of Representatives. He liked the role of House Spouse and had almost single-handedly defined it. He's been my biggest booster ever since the frigid January day in 1973 when I stood under that pristine white dome with my right hand in the air, being sworn into the Ninety-third Congress with one thought overriding my excitement and pride: *What the hell am I doing here?* As one hand pledged allegiance to uphold the Constitution, the other was trying to corral my son and daughter. Six-year-old Scott had figured out that this ceremony was the longest, dullest event he'd ever been forced to attend and felt compelled to liven things up by prodding two-year-old Jamie into a toddler-sized frenzy. As the wind whipped my long hair into knots

and I wiped apple-juice dribbles from my coat, I was surely the world's most improbable-looking politico.

I was not supposed to be the politician in the family.
Ten years earlier, Jim, and I, clutching our twin Harvard
Law School diplomas, looked at a map and thought Colorado would be a congenial place to live. We moved there,
Jim entered a law practice, and I happily embraced the
kind of legal career that would eventually accommodate a
family. I practiced law in the Denver office of the National Labor Relations Board, one of the 1930s Roosevelt agencies that dealt with unions and management, where our
cases involved companies that refused to bargain with strik-
ing employees or might have violated the right to organize
the workforce. When our first child was born in 1966, I
had the luxury of giving up full-time employment and taking on, mostly at home, only those projects that sang to me.
I started doing pro bono work for two of my pet causes,
Rocky Mountain Planned Parenthood and Denver Fair
Housing Group. I became a hearing officer for the Colorado State Personnel Board; state employees with a griev-
ance had the right to a hearing. I listened to both sides and
then wrote a legal opinion. I approached politics only from
the safe perch and vantage point of a classroom, teaching
political science and constitutional law first at the University of Colorado, then at Regis College.

Jim worked for a small law firm that represented the
founders of Vail, at a time when the ski resort was being

created out of whole cloth, or whole mountain. Many clients offered early opportunities to invest in Vail. I said, "No deal—it's too cold and too far from Denver!" I couldn't imagine that the precipitous, inaccessible chunk of the Rockies would ever be that valuable. (Hah! There are more Monday morning quarterbacks in real estate than in sports.) Jim had taken one stab at local politics himself, losing the 1970 election for the statehouse by a mere forty-two votes, and he was all but precluded from running again because the Colorado state legislature redrew his district. Every ten years, after the national census, the Census Bureau sends new data to each state, which is mandated to make all the voting districts as equal in population as possible. (Ten years later, they'll be out of whack again.) But the people drawing the lines are state legislators, the people who run for office. Reapportioning legislative districts gives the wolves the chance to change the henhouse. In order to prevent Jim from making a second run and likely winning, the new district boundaries were drawn down a major street and literally around our house. On the map, our address was a little protrusion cut out of the old district and placed in a new one that didn't make any sense, except that's where Schroeder lived. There were only about eleven people from Jim's old territory included in the new one. But the law of unintended consequences bit the gerrymanderers—they kept Jim from running but they launched my political career!

My husband the politician was on an ad hoc committee looking for a candidate to run against the incumbent congressman from Denver's first district. James D. "Mike" McKevitt was the city's first Republican representative in a quarter century. Denver had traditionally sent at least one liberal Democrat to Washington to balance the rest of the state's congressional delegation, which was considered very reactionary. In 1970, McKevitt had rubbed out Denver's tiny progressive foothold. As the district attorney, he had closed down the soft-porn film *I Am Curious Yellow* and several restaurants with a hippie clientele, basically campaigning on the idea: We're going to get those scumbags out of here. For this, his first reelection, he was running on the same model. A state senator named Clarence "Arch" Decker was going to run on the Democratic ticket, but Jim and others were looking for an alternative to Decker. They thought he was really an elephant in donkey's clothing. (They were proven right: Some years later he changed parties and ran against me again.)

There was no roster of other amenable Democratic aspirants because in 1972 the national election looked so hopeless. People like to see *some* hope of winning before jumping into the race. The presidential candidate, George McGovern, had no coattails in the West; he was wearing the political equivalent of a bikini. Anyone good who was approached by the committee said no thanks, thinking it was a kamikaze run.

One night Jim came home from a committee meeting just as I had finished bathing the children and reading *Goodnight Moon* for the eight hundredth time. "Guess whose name came up for Congress?" he asked. I shrugged. "Yours," he said.

My first reaction was, "Don't tease me, I'm tired. Why should I be the designated kamikaze?"

But he was serious. "There's no way you'll ever win this thing," he said. "You probably can't even win the primary. But if you don't get in the race and articulate the issues, they will not be discussed. You think the government's policies about Vietnam and the environment are wrongheaded, and you're always urging your students to get involved. It's an opportunity that may not come again."

I wondered what they served at this meeting—was he nuts?

After some sleep and some more arm-twisting, I finally agreed. I was certain my candidacy was a well-meaning and short-lived exercise in futility. I'd be Doña Quixote! I announced my surprise candidacy in a downtown hotel, and almost immediately had a request from United Press International to photograph me holding my child—my *younger* child, the people there stipulated. The picture went everywhere. I'd never thought about being a candidate for anything. One day, three weeks later, I *was* one and now the world knew it.

My parents, who lived near us in the suburb of Aurora,

were on a three-week tour of Asia (my father sold aviation insurance and was part of a tour group put together by the state insurance commissioner). When they returned to find their daughter running for Congress, my mother wanted to have me tested for drugs.

We had to move fast because it was mid-April and party caucuses were in May. The lowest political denomination is the precinct where you vote, and in Colorado each party has a place where people in that precinct gather on caucus night to elect a delegate to the party's convention. They take straw votes on candidates, so that when the convention is held, their delegate votes for the candidate favored by the majority of people. We had just days to organize people to get to their precinct caucuses to vote for me.

We set up campaign headquarters in the basement of our big 1890s Victorian home, built during the silver boom in Denver. This was no paneled party room. It looked like something out of Charles Dickens, with a huge coal furnace, but it had a separate entrance and it was free. I was massively outspent by my opponent: My average campaign contribution was $7.50. All the Democratic party officials sided with State Senator Arch Decker, wearing his oh-so-clever "I'm an Arch Supporter" buttons. They had selected their guy, and were going to anoint him. They'd been good at scaring off any other contenders—anyone who considered running was told, "It looks really bad out there, and Decker deserves his turn." Imagine their horror when some uppity thirty-two-year-old woman challenged their imprimatur.

Only two elected Democrats endorsed me, State Representative Jerry Rose and State Senator George Brown, the only African-American elected officials in Colorado at that time. They didn't like the entrenched guys trying to lock up the party, and they knew Decker, whatever his party label, was to the right of Attila the Hun.

To make matters even more complicated, the Denver Democratic party chairman was my husband's law partner, Dick Young. He had come to the conclusion that the perfect standard-bearer for this election was Arch Decker: Yes, he was conservative, but he had a lot of his own money to spend so the party would not be severely squeezed. Party officials saw their job as preventing a primary. Here I was, upsetting their plan. Even worse, my campaign was reinforcing the antiwar message of McGovern. Why couldn't Jim control his wife? Jim had actually planned, and already started, to serve as campaign manager for his *other* law partner, Floyd Haskell, who was running for U.S. Senate. Floyd had been a Republican and changed parties over the Vietnam War, so this was a big-deal campaign. Suddenly, Jim had to change course, becoming the de facto manager of my tiny effort and Haskell's chances would have been hurt statewide by being aligned with the young Denver upstarts.

When I actually won the primary, with 55 percent of

the vote, the only person more shocked than I was Arch Decker. He went into a massive pout, literally pulling down the blinds in his house and refusing to speak to the press. (He "couldn't be reached for comment," said the *Denver Post*.) There was a pretty stunned look on my mother's face too, in the photograph of us on the front page of the *Post*. My first instinct was to say, "I didn't mean it. Can I go home now?" I had a lovely life—why would I want to give it up? Actually, I wasn't too worried, because everyone knew I couldn't win the general election. I felt I just had to suck it up and continue the chaos a little longer.

But I was jazzed by McKevitt, who thought he was going to waltz through a non-campaign to victory. With only six weeks between the primary and the general election, I needed a real campaign manager to supplement Jim's effort. I called Larry Wright, a friend from the National Labor Relations Board, who had served on the committee that drafted me. "You got me into this," I reproved, "and you've got to help me out." We moved campaign headquarters out of the basement and rented an ancient abandoned drugstore that looked like the place where Jimmy Stewart worked as a kid in *It's a Wonderful Life*. The sign was still hanging out front, but all the inventory was gone, and the building itself was on its last legs; it was torn down after we left. We used orange crates for desks and filing cabinets. (The day after the election, the man who owned the Denver Broncos came to see me and couldn't find a place to sit. We gave him a crate and said, "Pretend it's a bleacher seat.")

Much of the campaign emanated from the table in our dining room, a space so large our kids learned to ride bikes there. When PBS came to shoot some film for a political documentary, the slick media professionals could hardly believe my ragtag bunch. Two years before, McKevitt had defeated a young lawyer named Craig Barnes, largely on the issue of busing, but during that campaign Barnes had gotten a lot of idealistic people excited, and he generously turned over this energized grassroots group to me. There was a small organization in place, and my college students were ready to volunteer. One of them drove me around town in a Volkswagen Beetle. Other friends were young professionals who had just begun to contribute to cultural causes like the symphony and could write $100 checks for a political crusade that got them fired up. Some of my campaign workers had been in a church choir with Judy Collins and persuaded her to come for a fundraiser. Quickly I built a team. My juices were flowing. I figured I couldn't win, but I sure wanted to show.

A friend in advertising, Arnie Grossman, and his partner, Chuck Bartholomew, came up with the slogan, "She wins, we win." (The two of them would come over with their latest brilliant idea sketched out on storyboards, and Jamie would spill milk all over them. This was not a textbook campaign.) They designed posters addressing what I thought were the three most important issues of the campaign. One was a hard-hitting message about Vietnam showing gravestones in a military cemetery, captioned with a quote from one of President Nixon's speeches: "Yes, many of our troops have already been withdrawn." Another poster showed a small child sitting under a crucifix on a dirt floor in a migrant labor camp, with the caption: "This radical troublemaker is out to get something from us . . . Hope." The third big issue involved the possibility of Colorado hosting the Olympic games. I thought the Olympics was a wonderful and noble tradition, but the organizers had no way to bankroll all the facilities Colorado would need. The necessary infrastructure would drain the public funds, and we'd be paying for it ad infinitum. I had a poster made showing a little old lady walking down the street with a cane, captioned, "Cheer up, the Olympics are coming." It infuriated the men in Chamber of Commerce blazers who were glibly stretching the truth in their glossy solicitations around the world to bring the games to our state.

There was a local law prohibiting the display of political posters in yards, but there was no rule about windows or doors, so we plastered the neighborhoods. Then we had the posters made into postcards and asked supporters to send them to five friends. Arnie knew how to buy paper wholesale, and the posters cost about a penny apiece, which was fortunate since we had almost no money. I didn't want to run up any debt that I'd be stuck with when I lost on Election Day.

Often I was ready to exhale and return to life as we knew it on earth—and then my opponent would say something that fired me up again. My one trip to Washington seeking financial help was a disaster. As a neophyte in politics, I didn't understand that ducking the issues was the goal of most campaigns. I actually thought I was supposed to deal with them! The head of the Democratic Congressional Campaign Committee took one look at my posters and roared, "Surely these haven't hit the street yet." I was informed that a *real* candidate would "discuss" issues, but not boldly take sides. They wanted lyrical brochures filled with photos of my family posing on the Capitol steps, sitting in front of the fireplace—every predictable, hackneyed, bowdlerized political image I'd ever scoffed at.

When Shirley MacLaine came to Colorado on her whistle-stop tour for McGovern, she helped emphasize one of the central points of my campaign: the breakdown in communication between government and the public. At a store in Boulder, she passed out copies of a statement from Nixon's consumer adviser, Virginia Knauer, whose response to inflationary grocery prices was "Just shop harder." I had many ideas for how Congress could be better in touch with the issues important to constituents. I got Denverites to send in their property tax stubs to demonstrate to Congress the need for tax relief.

Ironically, I became best known for supporting the lettuce boycott. This was an important issue for the large Chicano population of the city. I got it some well-deserved attention at the state Democratic party convention. Each candidate gets a certain number of minutes to address the delegates, but when I got up to speak, the party officers forgot that rule. They decided that the way to handle me was to declare, "You have thirty seconds." I knew they were trying to use their muscle to muzzle me with their fast clock. I also knew *they* were in control. I couldn't think of anything to say in that limited time except "I support the lettuce boycott" and glared at the heavies. The audience roared and I got the most convention votes.

Gloria Steinem, who had just founded *Ms.* magazine, had never laid eyes on me, but she came to stump for me in Denver. When I picked her up at the airport myself in the family car, she must have thought: *What kind of rummy outfit is this?* But she was like the Energizer bunny for my campaign. A good friend loaned us her house for a fund-raising party, and people were climbing over the gates to get in—there was so much debris from so many guests that we had to have the lawn vacuumed the next day. At one point I went into an upstairs bedroom, and the guys from my campaign staff who hadn't been keen on Gloria's coming were sitting on the bed gleefully counting piles of cash that she had coaxed out of people's wallets. Women whose husbands fell in love with Gloria on sight vowed to go out and get aviator glasses.

In her speech, Gloria emphasized that women should vote for me because I was antiwar and for broad social programs, not out of feminist allegiance to another woman. But that was hardly a concern; a *Denver Post* poll reported that my candidacy was more of a threat to women voters than to men. The consensus, even from some of my most liberal friends, was that I was trying to do too much too fast. One of my great disappointments was the National Women's Political Caucus that I helped found in 1970. It didn't support me because the people running it thought it was too early for a woman to run for Congress! They asked me to build momentum slowly. "We don't have any women on the city council or the school board," one of the leaders said. "Why don't you try that?" I thought I'd have the support of certain issue-focused groups, but they could not get past my gender. Even though I'd worked at the National Labor Relations Board, the unions sent me a whopping $50 check. Environmentalists were so engaged in fighting the Olympics, they considered me a low priority for their limited resources of time or money.

But getting rejected by the establishment was the best thing that could have happened. Instead of listening to the slick advice of the high-paid pros, I stayed with the instincts of friends gathered at our house; we called it "kitchen table media." I think the voters responded to my directness. It seemed to penetrate the normal clutter and noise of politics.

My greatest asset was my opponent, who mostly chose to ignore me. I'd been trying to see McKevitt for a year before the election to talk about the Vietnam War. He answered my requests for a meeting by sending me a calendar, then a photograph of himself. He also sent a book about caring for infants when Jamie was born (I decided I'd rather follow my pediatrician's advice) and an agricultural yearbook (so help-ful for a city-dweller). Finally there was a newsletter featur-ing a front-page photo of him with an adorable Dalmatian puppy he was giving to local firemen. He had a great PR machine, funded by the taxpayers. After my primary victory, he started referring to me as "Little Patsy" (although I was several inches taller) in the few debates he agreed to have, and he dispatched a group of young women called "Mike's girls," dressed alike in plaid skirts, whose job was to bubble about what a "great guy" he was. They looked like real peri-od pieces and were decimated in the press.

I didn't realize until much later the significance of run-ning a campaign during the era of "dirty tricks." One day, while I was giving a speech, I looked out the window and saw a blue van pull up next to my car on the street. I ran outside, and the van sped away. But it wasn't the first time I had noticed something fishy. The glove compartment of my car showed signs of being rifled, and someone had broken into our house, although nothing seemed to be missing. A few years later a man named Timothy Redfern was arrested in Denver and told the police, "I'm the one the FBI hired to break into Pat Schroeder's house." I read about this in the newspaper—a rather interesting news item to encounter over your first cup of coffee. Under the Freedom of Information Act, I demanded my FBI file and discovered all sorts of things in those sixty pages. The Bureau had been paying Jim's barber to be an informer. (In hindsight, it did seem rather odd how often he would show up in the middle of dinner.) Redfern had broken in several times and taken such all-important secret documents as my dues statement from the League of Women Voters and one of my campaign buttons. (Doesn't "She wins, we win" sound like a Communist slogan?) The FBI had also been tracking my staff, who were occasionally invited to speak on college campuses about how impeachment worked.

As a taxpayer, I was outraged. The FBI could have had campaign buttons or found out I belonged to the League of Women Voters and other organizations merely by dropping by my campaign headquarters. To think it spent money to "steal" this information and find out what we ate for dinner showed how paranoid J. Edgar Hoover and his agency were. It also reminded me I was under a magnifying glass twenty-four hours a day.

Stepping into the polling booth on the morning of Election Day, pulling that lever to close the curtain behind me and casting a vote for myself, was a real Rocky Mountain high—particularly seeing my own name on the same ballot as George McGovern (and, unfortunately, Richard Nixon). After the polls closed at seven o'clock, Jim and I went to the drugstore to thank all my campaign workers, then to the Democratic headquarters at a hotel in Denver. Soon it was time to get in the car and go to the local TV stations for brief appearances on the ten o'clock news. By the time we got home, early numbers were showing me as the front-runner. At 2:00 A.M., wondering if we had veered off into the Twilight Zone, Jim drove to the Denver Election Commission, sure that the press reports of my victory were wrong.

They were right. I'd won with 52 percent of the vote.

Jim and I were awake all night, contemplating the enormity of what lay ahead. But we'd promised the kids a vacation, no matter what the outcome, so the day after the election, with reporters camped outside our front door, we scurried out the back to a cab waiting in the alley and went to Disneyland. What better place to regroup and plan ahead than Tomorrowland?

Leafing through a magazine on the plane, Jim found a quiz on how much change a person could absorb in one year, the total score determining whether survival was feasible. We failed flamingly, and the recommendation was institutional commitment.

Life had been too tumultuous for too long, but no rest was in sight. I had a strong desire for a settled nest, so we called a realtor in Virginia and said, "Find a house." When he located one in an unchic suburb, Jim flew out, bought it and came back in one day. We still live in that house, a red brick split-level on a cul-de-sac, and it still looks as if it was purchased over the phone. We bought our carpet, drapes and two cars by phone too. A Denver car dealer almost refused to deal with me. "Look, lady," he said, "no one picks out a car by phone. Don't you want to test-drive it?" When I told him I didn't have time, he said, "Well, what color do you want?" I assured him any color would do, and he just sputtered, "How can you not care?" We were constantly assuring salesclerks that our calls were not pranks—they seemed unfamiliar with customers saying, "If you can't have the color I'd like by the day I need it, then install what you have." But we delighted shop-keepers because our urgency allowed them to dump mer-chandise that hadn't sold. That's how we ended up with bright red shag carpet throughout the house and avocado kitchen appliances. We had noodled and fussed over every detail of our prior homes, combing through everything from decorator magazines to flea markets to find the per-fect accoutrements to our Silver Rush mansion. Now this new place smacked of desperation and time constraints.

But it was a nest, our nest, and we settled in. My fam-ily might have wanted June Cleaver installed in the kitchen, and I could have used her too. But there's fiction and there's function. Our house functioned for kids, dogs, rabbits, ponies and parents. The question remained: How would I function in that other House, the one on Capitol Hill?

2

Congressional Bull****

When I pulled my beige station wagon into the garage of the Rayburn Office Building five days before my swearing-in, the briefcase next to me on the front seat was smaller than the case of diapers, a preferred local Denver brand not available in the capital.

"Would you believe I'm a newly elected member of Congress?" I asked the parking attendant.

"No," he replied with a sullen gaze. "Leave your keys in the ignition."

It was not an unusual reaction. One of only fourteen women in Congress, I felt as if I had broken into and entered a private club. Most of my new colleagues considered me a mascot or a novelty, as if Denver voters had mistakenly thought "Pat" meant "Patrick," or else they assumed that Jim was the congressman. He grew weary of saying, "No, it's *her*." We had to smile through a sophomoric skit at the Denver Law Club, showing Jim with an apron and broom. Even the first Speaker of the House I served with, Carl Albert of Oklahoma, congratulated him when we first met. Some members blurted out, "Why didn't *you* run?" but Jim had a great "gotcha" response: "We ran the strongest candidate." You could hear necks snap and jaws drop. They probably thought the high altitude of Denver had affected us, and they were certain I'd be out the next term. One senior member of Congress said to me, "Politics is about thousand-dollar bills, Chivas Regal, Learjets and beautiful women. So what are you doing here?" I gave the dumbest possible answer, way beyond his ken: "Because I care about the issues." He looked at me as if I were mad.

Right after the election, all the new congressmen and -women had gathered in Washington for an "organizing period," and lots of them hung around to schmooze, but I didn't have much schmoozing time. I had given notice for December 31 at my various jobs, and I still had decisions to write for the Personnel Board and papers to grade for my students. Jim was closing down his law practice; his partner Floyd Haskell had also won election to the Senate. The third partner was John Tweedy, whose wife had decided she wanted to breed horses. When two of the horses turned out to be Secretariat and Riva's Ridge, they started thinking that this little hobby was going to be their retirement plan, and so they also moved to Virginia. Jim's firm was as much in the throes of change as every other part of our lives.

With our lives in chaos, I couldn't be in Washington when office assignments were determined by lottery. The House doorkeeper at the time, a character named "Fishbait" Miller, said he'd draw an office for me. I got number 1313. Not exactly an auspicious beginning, and when I saw the place, it was hard not to suspect sabotage. Number 1313 was way at the back of the Longworth House Office Building, the worst possible location and configuration: It was as far away as it could be from the House floor and still be in the District. Each congressperson was entitled to three rooms, but my third room was off on another floor so I had to use Pony Express to reach my staff. The office furniture was early Men's Club: heavy, dark, and ugly. The whole place cried out for a moth-eaten moose head and a spittoon. To brighten up the office, we painted the skyline of Denver on one wall. That turned out to be a huge no-no: From the official response I got, you would have thought I'd driven my car down the hall.

There were four other women starting congressional careers along with me: Barbara Jordan (Democrat from Texas); Elizabeth Holtzman (Democrat from New York), who was a year behind me in law school; Yvonne Brathwaite Burke (Democrat from California) and Marjorie Holt (Republican from Maryland). Within months, two more women inherited the House seats of husbands who died in plane crashes: Cardiss Collins (Democrat from Illinois) and Corinne Claiborne "Lindy" Boggs (Democrat from Louisiana). A high percentage of the early women in Congress got there that way. The senior woman at that time was Leonor Sullivan (Democrat from Missouri), who saw herself more as the standard-bearer of her husband, the fallen leader, than as a leader in her own right. She often called herself "Mrs. John."

The other tradition of women in the House followed two tracks: Either it was a capstone at the end of a career for those with grown children, or it *was* the career for unmarried or childless women. You could have a career or a family, or maybe a career *after* your family was grown. But rearing a family while being in Congress was unheard of. I'd never met Bella Abzug, the Democratic congresswoman from New York and America's premier feminist, so our first contact after my election was rather surprising. "I hear you have little kids," she said. "You won't be able to do this job." Eventually we became friends, and after her unsuccessful run for the Senate, when her political career was spiraling down, I used to say, "I wish I could just *buy* Bella a seat and get her back here." It broke my heart to see her looking at suburban districts where she might find a new constituency, when she was obviously born to represent New York City. (Tip O'Neill once stumped for her and said, "I think she's to the right of her district.") Often she was so caught up in the righteousness of her position, and so assured of her passion, that she didn't believe anybody else had the same commitment, and it turned people off. Many male colleagues just wanted to stay out of her wake. "You could always tell Bella, but you couldn't tell her much," they said. She never hesitated to roll over people—she didn't give a rat's ass who she offended for a righteous cause. She was the classsic Type A New Yorker you pray is on your side. Once when she was trying to strategize a return to politics, she called me for help and then started yelling that there was no voice for women in the House. I thought: *You're asking for my help, and you just insulted me.* Still, I love her passion. You can't buy her.

Lindy Boggs was Abzug's opposite: a real Southern lady, totally nonthreatening, without a trace of cattiness. Her daughter, the TV reporter Cokie Roberts, once said to me, "Mother is the type of woman who if she found her husband under the covers with another woman would say 'Oh my, they must have been cold.'" During the Watergate era, she was hesitant to criticize the president, politely stating that we ought to wait to condemn him. Her husband, Hale Boggs, had been the majority leader, so she inherited a huge staff. She was not about making waves. She'd go to some conference and say very politely what should be done about women's rights and just be *thrilled.* But for her generation, she was flaming *out* there—and quite effective with our male colleagues who had an awful time saying no to her.

I'm amazed Patsy Mink, the exuberant, intelligent and outgoing Democrat from Hawaii, ever got involved in politics. During World War II, the U.S. would call Japanese Americans for a lineup, and many were shipped away to internment camps. She lived through that ugly part of American history, which may be what caused her to run for office: to make sure such events never happen again. My theory about Hawaii is that it's always been a more progressive state on women's issues because it has been ruled by a queen. (Hawaii also elected Pat Saiki, a moderate Republican, to the House, and she went on to be the head of the Small Business Administration under George Bush.) The cost of living there has always been high, so there were more women in the workplace earlier than on the mainland. Patsy was a DES mother—while trying to get pregnant and carry to term, she'd taken diethylstilbestrol, the drug that was later found to cause horrible birth defects and disease—so she was always passionate and informed about all women's health issues.

One of my earliest memories in the House was listening to Patsy eloquently defending Title IX, which required gender equity in public education. We were congratulating her after her speech when she got a phone call that her only daughter, Wendy, had been in a horrible car crash. She left immediately, and obviously did not vote. The next day there was an article in the *New York Times* questioning her competency for "forgetting" to vote. We wrote searing letters to the paper, outraged that the editors had never bothered to inquire why she was absent—they just attacked. When Congress was voting on the Equal Rights Amendment, Hawaii kept a plane running at National Airport because it wanted to rush the bill to Hawaii and be the first state to ratify the ERA. Little did it know no other state was vying for the privilege.

Shirley Chisholm was more formal, reserved, traditional. Her heritage was Caribbean, and she was almost British in her style, her caution and her organization. A former teacher, Shirley lit up like a lightbulb any time she was within ten feet of a child. A group of African-American children once told her that the White House should be called the Polka Dot House—a more multicultural theme. She loved it. She was a real leader, and I worked hard to get her elected chair of the Democratic Caucus. "Give a woman a chair" was our slogan. We lost, but she came back to support any children's cause worth fighting for and helped me campaign in Denver.

Edith Green (Democrat from Oregon) rattled my optimism about women in politics. A power in the House Education Committee, she had been Bobby Kennedy's campaign manager in the west and was considered a progressive until she hit upon the issue of busing, to which she was vehemently, rabidly opposed. The mother of the antibusing movement was a Boston housewife named Louise Day Hicks, who got elected to Congress in 1970 and defeated in '72, after too much exposure for her outrageous opinions. (According to one story, the Education Committee went to Los Angeles, where many of the people attending a hearing were Hispanic. Hicks looked around and said something like, "How did all these Puerto Ricans get this far?") Edith Green wasn't that dumb, but everyone loves a liberal who's gone south, and she rode to power on the school bus, becoming quite the prima donna. She did not like me and threatened to campaign with one of my Republican opponents. A senior male colleague told me, "Don't worry—that lady is no gentleman."

Olympia Snowe (Republican from Maine) is a class act and steady as a rock—when she came to Congress a few years after I did, she reminded me of the person who heads the prom committee in high school. Her level-headed composure must have helped her endure the tragedies of her life: She was widowed when she came to Congress. We were all excited when she married the governor of her state, but soon after their marriage, his son died in an athletic accident at Dartmouth, the young victim of undiagnosed heart disease. As if those tragedies weren't enough to deal with, those early years were hard times to be Republican if you cared about women's issues, as Olympia did and does. One of her pet projects was getting research funding for osteoporosis. Most Republicans in the White House had a dismal record of supporting women's causes. She campaigned very hard for George

Bush, since one of the sixteen places he calls home is Maine. I'm sure she had to be very disappointed when he refused to meet with the caucus she and I cochaired the entire four years he was in office. She thought he'd be much bettter on women's issues than Reagan, but it wasn't so. I bet she wished she could recoup all that campaigning she did for him.

Margaret Heckler (Republican from Massachusetts) is a Catholic and was divorced while in office. Divorce in the public eye is no fun—all of it plays out in the local papers, and I knew whatever she was going through was not pretty. It continued to cause difficulties for her, especially when she went on to become the ambassador to Ireland. Republicans from Massachusetts are more progressive than most Democrats from other states, but she often felt under siege as the only woman in a rough-and-tumble delegation. Massachusetts hasn't sent a woman to Congress since she was defeated by Barney Frank.

When Martha Griffiths (Democrat from Michigan) left Congress, we lost the mother of the Equal Rights Amendment. She came from the old-fashioned school of politics as public service and was not in the least interested in becoming a Washington power broker, golfing with the guys who controlled the war chests or being feted at $1,000-a-plate dinners. She fattened her campaign coffers with a once-a-year pancake breakfast in her district. But her husband, Hicks, was in poor health, and she returned to Michigan, winning election as lieutenant governor. Had she stayed in the House, she would have been the most senior member of the Ways and Means Committee and would have become its chairman when Wilbur Mills left instead of Dan Rostenkowski. Ways and Means became famous for its preferential treatment of high rollers, granting favorites little "bennies" like tax breaks. Martha wouldn't have stood for such favors. Ways and Means would have been a very different place under her leadership.

Millicent Fenwick (Republican from New Jersey) was an original. Her parents were very wealthy and died when the ship they were on sank. She was reared by private tutors in a swish part of the state where the houses are the size of hotels. She smoked a pipe and dressed in the grand tweeds-and-pearls style of *Vogue*, where she'd once been an editor. She'd dismissively talk about how old her clothes were—never mind that you could have bought a car for the price of one of her suits. I felt like an unmade bed when I was around her.

Millicent's patrician background sometimes made her seem out of touch: Once when we were discussing legislation to protect the handicapped, she mumbled something about most people keeping the disabled on the third floor of their house, with staff. And when we were discussing survivors' rights to foreign service officers' pensions, she said that her sister was married to a foreign service officer, and *she* certainly didn't need the money. It was hard to convince her that for most people such a job was not hobby farming—they needed the money. But she felt free to tell her party off on the issue of abortion and many other issues. When she was with us, she lent great gravitas to the debate.

Another from the best-dressed list was Geraldine Ferraro (Democrat from New York—does anyone not know that?). She represented Archie Bunker's neighborhood in Queens. When she arrived in the mid-1970s, full of spunk, we worked together to enact our dream of making the federal government the nation's model employer. For one brief and shining moment were able to pass a passel of legislation on flexi-time, staggered work schedules, equal pay for equal work and job-sharing. We really brought those work and family issues into the language and the public's sensibilities by the end of the '70s. When Walter Mondale chose her as his vice presidential running mate, I was thrilled. (I myself would probably not be a good vice president. I think it's a tough job, like being the Prince of Wales. Your life is not your own, your hands are not on the content—and I'm not a good cheerleader.) But Gerry's candidacy was such an important seed-planter in the minds of young women and girls, a wonderful example of their limitless possibilities. She was great on television and never wilted under fire.

It was certainly logical and appropriate that the women in Congress would all be so different, but the result was no sense of a cohesive unit. Obviously we were more powerful together than separate. Marjorie Holt was stuck behind her "I am not a women's libber" platitudes, and "Mrs. John's" attitude was: Who needs you? By 1975, with more pressure coming to bear from outside women's groups, we finally were able to start the bipartisan Congressional Women's Caucus, under the chairmanship of Liz Holtzman and Peggy Heckler. But to do it we all put handcuffs on ourselves: The older women didn't want to be embarrassed by the new firebrands, so we had to agree that there be unanimous consent on any issue before we acted and no more than $50 in annual dues. In 1980, when Holtzman and Heckler both ran for the Senate (and both lost), Olympia Snowe and I became cochairs. We decided the group was mature enough to run by majority rule and upped the dues to $2,500. And we let men in, renaming ourselves the Caucus on Women's Issues. But the men paid much lower dues, and we basically said, "We'll tell you what the issues are. Have a nice day."

Anyone watching how the new men in Congress were socialized could see the differences immediately: The senior bulls picked out younger bulls who were like them in ideology and attached themselves as guides and mentors. The only woman who enjoyed some camaraderie from her male colleagues was Barbara Jordan, who had been in the Texas state legislature and had worked with many of the men in her delegation. The Texans were a wild bunch with a club mentality. They had their own table in the congressional dining room with their own bottles of hot sauce, and they all wore cowboy boots and sang songs and howled at the moon. I was utterly jealous. My own Colorado colleagues, a tiny delegation of five, were kind of stunned by my arrival — the first woman ever to represent our state in Congress. My hospitality committee consisted of the congressman from Pueblo, Frank Evans, who sent one of his staff over to show my staff how to fill out forms.

The women in Congress had to wage virtually every battle alone, whether we were fighting for female pages (there were none) or a place where we could pee. The assumption was that we should be so appreciative of being allowed into the hallowed halls of Congress, we'd fall on our knees in gratitude for every crumb. There were men's bathrooms right off the main floor of the House, but the ladies' room was at the other end of the earth, constructed out of the original Speaker's lobby in the old Capitol, and it looked as if it hadn't been updated since the inception of indoor plumbing. Every now and then we would luck out when there was a visiting female dignitary, and the authorities had to spruce it up a bit. I never thought I would be cheering royalty (my Irish father had hung a plaque over our fireplace that read, "We owe allegiance to no king"), but when Queen Elizabeth II visited, we finally got some new curtains and paint in the ladies' room. I wonder what would have happened if the Queen had strayed onto the outdoor porch off the House chamber. The first time I wandered out there for some fresh air during a debate, I could hear a lot of *harrumphing* behind me. It seems that the congressmen liked to pull off their trousers and sunbathe on the chaise longues. They felt "letting" women on the House floor was enough; we shouldn't also have access to their tanning clinic.

Not being a Nixon favorite, I was not on the president's White House guest list. By tradition, he was forced to include me on one occasion, when all the freshmen in Congress were invited to 1600 Pennsylvania Avenue. I was eager to check out America's best public housing. The early spring evening was quite warm, but there were fires blazing in every hearth, and the air conditioners were turned on full blast. I was told that the president liked fires regardless of the temperature.

When I saw Nixon up close, I noticed he was wearing makeup in an orange shade that had streaked and caked, and I had an incredible urge to wash his face. I mentioned this to a newsman, who took me aside and confirmed that ever since the 1960 debates, when Nixon sweated and

Kennedy glowed, the president had been applying Man-Tan pancake and powder. I thought it was frightening—it reminded me of the stories about Queen Elizabeth I's last years on the English throne, her makeup getting more extreme as she became more out of touch. Every day there were new Watergate revelations on the front page of the *Washington Post*. I think Nixon was losing his grip on reality. He even had tried to put the White House guards in comic operatic outfits, like something out of *H.M.S. Pinafore*. I guess his theory was: If the place looked regal enough, then the rubbish wouldn't stick to it.

Jim and I chased Henry Kissinger all over the first floor of the White House trying to get him to answer questions about Vietnam policy, but he was arrogant and dismissive, just brushing us away like mosquitoes. The Department of Defense was widely known at the time for its "five o'clock follies." It held press conferences saying, "We're winning," and, "It's almost over," expecting us to swallow its line and defer to its experts. Then, an hour or two later, their experts would get creamed on the TV news by reporters who'd gone into the jungles of southeast Asia and found out the truth. I'd met with Joan Baez, who was using her folk music to rally the antiwar effort, and was haunted by photographs she showed me from North Vietnam. The United States was bombing day and night, anything that wiggled. Our next-door neighbor in Virginia worked at the Pentagon, responsible for shipments of bombs and ammunition to Vietnam. Even he was shattered by the tonnage he sent. One wondered if anything could live after so much lethal destruction was unleashed.

I had the temerity to mention all of this — Nixon's make-up, Kissinger's hubris — in a letter to a few of my close Denver supporters. A "friend" leaked the letter, provoking a series of editorials in the Denver press that charged me with impertinence and irreverence and not being sufficiently circumspect. I learned the hard way: Whoever's got the best gossip has power, and that drives one's temptation to "leak." My three rules of politics became quickly established: (1) Don't lie. (2) Don't do anything you don't want to read about on the front page. (3) If you do, go back to rule one.

There were days I thought I was on the Mississippi River because of all the showboating in Congress. We were 435 class presidents, unleashed into the world beyond high school. Everyone was so afraid of becoming a follower that no one agreed with anyone else. People stole each other's bills and reintroduced them, rather than cosponsoring them. We dealt with such pressing issues as whether it was legal to fly a kite in the District and whether policemen would allow firemen to play in their band.

A month after I arrived in Congress, I was asked to speak at a convention of the National Women's Political

Caucus (NWPC) in Houston, a historic event. It was the first time such a group of political women had convened in more than one hundred years. I boarded an evening flight for Houston with Shirley Chisholm, but mechanical trouble forced us to land in Atlanta and spend hours on the runway, waiting for repairs. A freakish blizzard was predicted for Houston, and the authorities thought we had a better chance of beating the storm if we stayed on the plane. When we finally got to Houston the next morning, four inches of fresh snow covered the ground, and our Texas hosts, unaccustomed to such weather, were too alarmed about driving to collect us at the airport. Shirley and I rented a car and drove ourselves to the Rice Hotel. We would have ridden on the backs of armadillos if necessary—it was such an exciting time. The Equal Rights Amendment had passed through Congress and was awaiting ratification by the individual states. We felt victory was preordained. The women in politics were heady with new-found potential, like babies discovering their fingers and toes. Almost every state had an NWPC affiliate, and lots of women were thinking: *Maybe I should run for office.*

But the soaring optimism of that meeting soon turned to feelings of siege when we got back to the real world. The right wing found an effective countermeasure, marshaling its female forces in opposition to ERA and creating a stalemate. Much of what ERA opponents did was theater. They paraded around with big red octagonal signs that said STOP ERA, asking why women would want to share public toilets or wear combat boots, or destroy their secure marriages. "Don't we all love the privilege of having men take care of us?" they asked. In Cleveland, a group called Ladies Against Women, wearing gloves and pillbox hats, donned buttons that said "I'd rather be ironing," and they responded to the statistic that women earned only fifty-nine cents of a man's dollar in salary by carrying placards that said "59 cents is enough."

The usual format for TV coverage was to pit one of the Houston bunch against one of the Stepford Wives wearing pink and looking cute. It was always a sporting event, like two cats fighting. Seldom was there any substantive discussion about what this amendment would actually do. Most men and many women tuned out the debate. The inclusion of women was not viewed as a civil rights cause. Many male policy-makers reacted as if women were some monolithic entity. They felt they could ignore our issues until we spoke with a unanimous voice. The far right sent the Phyllis Schlaflys of the world out to be sure we never looked unanimous.

———

Much of my time was spent trying to master the rules and procedures of the House. It often seemed so stilted and obtuse. But I also spent a lot of time learning about other sets of rules, the unwritten ones of the guy gulag. Those were even harder to ascertain.

The House cloakroom is a traditional off-the-floor hangout, a cloakroom with no coat hooks. Originally, congressional offices were not connected to the House floor by tunnel, and it must have been too far to walk back for a meeting, but now the cloakroom is more of a feeding trough, an L-shaped space with a woman making sandwiches at a lunch counter, lots of phone booths and ugly dark brown chairs in front of a TV. On nights when Congress went late, there were great battles over what got watched. Once there was a PBS special on suffragettes, but the men wanted to watch basketball. One of the other congresswomen got the clicker and sat on it. (We watched the special, but you could cut the tension with a knife. Unwritten Rule Number One: Guys control the cloakroom clicker!)

In 1972 Title IX had just passed, ensuring that any institution getting public funding had to offer the same programs to men and women, and athletics took a big hit. A lot of men acted like women were breaking into the locker room. At one Denver high school I visited, the coach told the basketball team, "Show Mrs. Schroeder what you think of Title Nine," and they turned around and mooned me.

It was in that atmosphere of enmity that I found myself in the mid-1970s at the Touchdown Club, a Washington brotherhood of businessmen who are jock wannabes and throw a black-tie dinner with sports celebrities every year. One of my colleagues, Congressman Charlie Rose (Democrat from North Carolina), bought two tickets, then found out he couldn't go and offered them to me. I knew Jim would love an evening with the jockocracy. We got all dressed up in formal wear. To our great surprise, a guard who looked like a linebacker was standing at the door of the hotel blocking our way.

"No women allowed," he said in a no-nonsense voice.

"What are you talking about?" I asked.

A group of bouncers encircled us. "If you don't leave quietly," one of them said, "you'll be carried out."

I was speechless. The public accommodations law that passed in the 1960s, prohibiting discrimination in public places based on gender, race or religion, covered exactly this kind of event. Had I been asked to leave because I was black or Jewish, my colleagues would have been outraged. This was just a woman thing. That night I discovered Unwritten Rule Number Two, that many of my colleagues liked Washington as a female-free zone. I will never forget their faces, laughing as we were shown the door. Someone even asked Jim why he "let" me do this, as if he was a traitor to the club. It galls me now that I left willingly. Perhaps I should have been more Rosa Parks–like and refused to budge, but it was clear they had the greater mass and would win. I later found out that a female reporter from *Time* magazine was denied entrance too, as was a woman whose father was getting an award that night. The unwritten rule was rigorously enforced. The public accommodations law was not.

(A heartening footnote: In 1996, apparently willing to join the twentieth century, albeit a bit late in the game, the Touchdown Club invited me to attend a dinner and presented me with one of its coveted Timmie awards for sportsmanship.)

But the Touchdown scrimmage was nothing compared to the fights I had within the Capitol. In a setup typical of Congress, where everything is done by committee, there is a committee to decide committee assignments for incoming freshmen. In 1973 it was headed by Representative Wilbur Mills of Arkansas. Most of the women in Congress took their assignments without protest. Shirley Chisholm, elected two years before I was, had refused a position on the Agriculture Committee, stating the obvious fact that her Brooklyn district didn't have one farmer. She stated it *publicly* and generated such public furor and ridicule directed at Congress that she was finally appointed to Education and Labor, where a former teacher like Chisholm actually belonged. But Shirley was the exception.

Considering that no senior member was going to fall on his sword for me, I expected to be assigned to something like Merchant Marine and Fisheries. Since my Denver district is landlocked and doesn't have enough water to float a duck, it would have meant sudden death for a new congressional career. I wanted to be on the Armed Services Committee. I wanted to be part of the committee that controlled approximately sixty-five cents out of every dollar allocated to Congress. How could a group spending so much money—$80 billion that year—to protect women and children do so without the representation of a single woman?

The Armed Services chairman, F. Edward Hébert (pronounced A-Bear), was a seventy-two-year-old Louisiana Democrat who was dead set against my appointment. In one of our first conversations, he said to me, "I hope you aren't going to be a skinny Bella Abzug." What I didn't know was that Wilbur Mills really lobbied for me, over Hébert's roar. Even though Mills chaired the committee, I couldn't understand why he would override Hébert's veto. There was an unspoken rule that old congressional barons never cross each other. Obviously I was thrilled to be on Armed Services, and it wasn't until several years later that I was able to connect the dots. It turned out that Mills was driven by guilt to be my great advocate. Unbeknownst to me, Mills's wife had taken an interest in my career and apparently kept telling her husband that he should do whatever he could to help me. In 1974, the press found Mills wading in the Tidal Basin near the Jefferson Memorial with a stripper named Fanne Foxe. So his guilt over his relationship with Fanne Foxe must have made him much more prone to please his wife.

Mills, my anonymous benefactor, had performed the necessary arm-twisting.

For several years, I thought my appointment to Armed Services was on the merits. But then I learned Unwritten Rule Number Three: Things are rarely on the merits in Washington.

Although I was on the committee, I did not get a seat. Hébert was patronizingly contemptuous of women in politics (he inscribed a copy of his book, *Creed of a Congressman*, "For the House Armed Services Committee's first lovely den mother"). He also objected to the appointment of Congressman Ron Dellums (Democrat from California). Ron had been in the House only one term when it was decided that it was time for an African-American to be on the Armed Services Committee. Hébert didn't appreciate the idea of a girl and a black forced on him. He was outraged that for the first time a chairman's veto of potential members was ignored. He announced that while he might not be able to control the makeup of the committee, he could damn well control the number of chairs in his hearing room, where he was enthroned on a carpet of stars, surrounded by military flags. He said that women and blacks were worth only half of one "regular" member, so he added only one seat to the committee room and made Ron and me share it. Nobody else objected, and nobody offered to scrounge up another chair. Armed Services was the most powerful committee in Congress during the Vietnam War, and Hébert ran it like a personal fiefdom. Many of the other forty-two committee members had military bases in their districts and had a vested interest in pleasing the chairman, no matter how outrageous he was. They felt their political careers depended upon their being able to go home and tell their constituents, "Look how much money I got for you this year for our base."

Ron and I had two choices: to go ballistic or to hang in. We decided to hang. So we sat "cheek to cheek" on one chair, trying to retain some dignity. Once in a heated debate, Ron said to Hébert, "There are only two of us with the balls to stand up against what we all know is wrong." I tugged on his arm and suggested "balls" was not a precisely accurate description of our coalition. Years later my friend Barney Frank (Democrat from Massachusetts) said, "That was the only half-assed thing either of you ever did."

But our "half-assed thing" led to Hébert's undoing. Shortly after I was appointed, I tried to come to some sort of truce with Hébert. I paid a call on him in his office. He was the only congressman with a patio entrance and a seven-room suite, including an "adultery" room with nude paintings, a bar, a couch and no windows. There were hundreds of pictures of Hébert in his office, and one likeness etched in marble that he planned to use for a tombstone. Back in his Louisiana district, he had named streets, hospitals and other institutions after himself. He was an ego run amok. He had long ago lost all sense of the

Armed Services Committee as a democratically run body. "The Lord giveth and the Lord taketh away," he told me, "and here I am the Lord." He had outlived all rivals for the chairmanship and thought he was above challenge, literally stomping in fury if a junior member like me made a suggestion that diverged from his own considered opinion. "There are certain people who make me shudder," he once said, looking at me, "every time they open their mouth." No truce could be negotiated.

I thought the Constitution's system of checks and balances meant that Congress was to oversee other branches of government and act if they were out of control, but Armed Services under Hébert was just a mouthpiece for the military. We had the fewest number of staffers of any congressional committee—the attitude was, "What would we use them for?" The Pentagon justified its most extravagant costs with "The Russians are coming" logic: Either the Russians were doing it, so we had to keep up, or the Russians were not doing it, so we had to stay ahead. Oversight and analysis were not the committee's mission.

One of the first visitors to my own tiny quarters was John Wayne, who wanted to warn me about Commies. (Imagine, this little gnat, me, was such a worry to the hawks they sent John Wayne after me!) "I've sworn to uphold the Constitution," I countered. "Do you think I'm the weak link here?" He offered me a silver cigarette lighter engraved with the inscription, "Fuck communism—John Wayne." I was appalled and declined the gift, but my husband was furious, imagining its memorabilia value at a flea market. He reminds me of this incident about once a week.

I have to admit, I knew it would inflame Hébert when I insisted on exercising my right as a committee member and attached additional views to the annual defense budget bill. I accused the committee of being a Pentagon lapdog. There were many examples when committee members appeared annoyed or afraid of vigorous, open congressional debate about the military. But I didn't *just* mean to aggravate the chairman. Long after Hébert was gone—in fact, for as long as I served on the committee—I submitted supplemental reports about Pentagon practices. I published alternative defense budgets—suggesting that NATO allies contribute more, or pointing out that one weapon system worked but another was junk. Some of my colleagues would argue, "What does she know? She never served in the military." But most of them hadn't either. My staff and I called them "The Wimps of War." Hébert called me "the Colorado bomb thrower." Once when I questioned U.S. bombing raids on Cambodia, he said, "I wish you'd support our boys like you support the enemy," and when I voted to cut off funds for the continued bombing, he yelled, "No! That's the dumbest thing I ever heard."

I realized early on that I needed to be fully informed when I was challenging billions of dollars in Pentagon expenditures, sorting out the complex jargon of defense: Condor and Safeguard and Trident and Polaris. I thought it was crazy to feel secure in maintaining enough weaponry to annihilate an enemy fifteen times over instead of "only" five times. I thought it was crazy that the Trident submarine was sold to Congress because it was bigger and faster than the Polaris. Size and speed, while admirable qualities in another context, tend to make submarines more detectable because they make more noise—a fact I had the audacity to point out in an article for *The Nation*.

In the summer of 1973, Speaker Carl Albert appointed me to represent him at a disarmament conference on chemical and nerve gas stockpiles in Geneva, Switzerland. The conference was important to my district because a huge quantity of vintage nerve gas weapons left over from the Korean War was sitting in storage at the end of the Denver Stapleton Airport runway. The canisters were in clear view, and my worst nightmare was a terrorist in a small plane circling and threatening to crash into them unless his demands were met.

I had been pushing the military to do something about this potential disaster from my first day in Congress but never publicly. I was afraid mere mention of it might plant the idea in the mind of a lunatic who hadn't already thought of the opportunity. But pushing the military privately was a waste of time. Everyone I questioned gave me the same response: Our chemical weapons would not be destroyed unless the rest of the world did the same. One general even said, "Those canisters kept the Russians out of Denver, didn't they?" He would never have said such a thing publicly, but privately he could be insolent and condescending. Moving the bombs was impossible since no other state would take them. Every week when I flew back to Denver, I looked out the window of the plane at those stockpiles and shuddered for the safety of my city. The Geneva conference was pivotal because if the world did not agree to do something about the destruction of the global stockpile, our military would never move to detoxify Colorado's share.

House rules required that even though Speaker Albert appointed me, Chairman Hébert had to sign an order for me to be reimbursed for my travel expenses—strictly pro forma and rarely denied. He refused, responding to inquiries from the press by saying, "She'll get goodies when she behaves like the others." There was nothing he could do about my going to Geneva, other than preventing me from getting my expenses paid, but he went on to select Marjorie Holt to represent him. Freshmen were expected to be desperate to "go along" so they would look like "players" and their constituents would believe they had clout with the barons of Congress. Whacked by one of the bulls, I was supposed to lick my wounds and thereafter serve as a voluntary gofer for the whacker until I was forgiven. But I had no time for repentance or gofering. I went public.

I had always believed government was not a fungus: It

could survive in sunshine. I had buttons printed saying, "Help, I have Hébert by the tail" (and everyone in Congress knew to pronounce it "A-bear"). The reality, in terms of power, was the opposite, but I handed out the buttons to my colleagues, explaining the joys of sitting on half a chair and exposing his other boorish actions. Hébert's reaction was to mutter with disdain, "So you're going to be one of those cheap kind who'll do anything for publicity." *Redbook* magazine did a cover story on my challenge to the Old Guard, entitled "The Woman Who Has a Bear by the Tail" and calling me David to Hébert's Goliath. The account of his stiffing the Speaker and attempting to punish me contributed to the further unraveling of his power.

I decided that if I was going to the conference on my own dime, I'd make a vacation out of it. Jim and I bought cheap tickets to Luxembourg on Icelandic Airlines for the whole family, then rented a car and drove to Geneva. Marjorie Holt was flown in by the military, who carried her bags, opened her doors and paid her bills. There was a group of nations represented at the conference ready to sign treaties limiting stockpiles and demanding inspections, but the United States was not willing to do that—we were too worried about the Soviets. I had gone to Switzerland naively believing that good people will come to their senses, once given the right information, and when I realized that wasn't going to happen, I was galvanized to approach the problem a different way.

The effort begun at that conference is one of the proud-est acts of my career. It was a long process, but I got those bombs demilitarized and detoxified. I discovered that George B. Kistiakowsky, the science adviser to the Eisen-hower administration, was teaching at Harvard, and I went to ask him about the Denver stockpile. He nearly exploded. "Don't tell me those haven't been demilitarized?" he said in horror. He explained that the weapons were not preci-sion-made, and they'd been rushed and thrown together in an emergency, and the detonators got more unstable with age. He helped spread the word that I wasn't some hysteri-cal peacenik. My new credibility caused the military to stop playing games with me. I still have trouble believing the Rocky Mountain Arsenal is now a national wildlife refuge. By the early 1990s, the cleanup was not yet complete, but suddenly there were pairs of nesting eagles moving in, stak-ing their claim on a new homestead. We panicked, think-ing that they might become contaminated. But they thrived. We had fifty-five pairs of nesting eagles there in 1997. From one of America's most contaminated sites to a beautiful wildlife refuge in ten years. Progress is possible.

In 1973 the Middle East was a powder keg, with a devastat-ing potential to drain U.S. oil supplies. I kept remembering the novel *On the Beach*, which places the start of World War

III in the Mideast. Our European allies were not allowing us to refuel aircraft sent to the Middle East, feeling that the United States had tilted too much toward Israel. Only Portugal allowed us to land in the Azores. Congress would soon be asked to authorize more than $2 billion for new Israeli arms and more than $4 billion for new U.S. weapons. The Armed Services Committee decided to send a congressional delegation, called a "codel," to determine what Israel needed and how fast it needed it. The trip would last ten days and cover almost thirty thousand miles of flying, with twenty mostly older, male, conservative colleagues. The few other dissenting voices on the committee decided not to make the journey. The history of the more progressive types on Armed Services was that they preferred to make their points through press releases, rather than subjecting themselves to the extended company of such antagonists. I decided on mutual assured misery. When I boarded the air force plane, there was the *Redbook* issue at every seat featuring my war with Hébert. (I've never seen one *Redbook* on an air force plane since.) It was a long, lonely trip.

The plan was to spend one day in Athens adjusting to the time zone and getting briefed by the State Department. The city looked eerie and felt uneasy as we drove in from the airport. At our hotel we got stuck in an elevator for half an hour, but we just shrugged and concluded that Greece must be more third-world than we thought. One of our delegation asked, "Hasn't there been a lot of dissent here lately?" and our State Department host said, "There have been some students throwing apples, but we don't consider it serious."

About 3:00 A.M. we were roused from sleep and told that a military coup was taking place. We were instructed to pack quickly, taking care not to turn on any lights in the bathroom or go near the windows. We were led to an alley behind the hotel, loaded on buses and told to lie on the floor. The hotel was in Constitution Square, where the government buildings were located, and it was encircled by tanks. Against orders, I did get off the floor to peek out the front window of the bus. The top of a tank opened and out came a banana peel—I guess even revolutionaries have to eat. I remember wondering what the Greek words were for "Don't litter." Before dawn, we were driven to the airport and hurried out of town.

It was the Jewish Sabbath, and no planes were supposed to land in Israel, but we got some special dispensation for escaping a military coup. In our Jerusalem hotel, doors were propped open and food left on buffet tables so that the hotel staff did not have to labor on the Sabbath.

For Americans, whose wars in this century have been so far away, Israel was amazing: Danger was so *close*. The war was just miles away from any citizen's front door. Its presence could be heard, seen and felt, even as the Israelis struggled to have life be as normal as possible. I was so surprised—and impressed—by that.

And I was struck by the fact that the entire country was on alert, but the upper echelons of government still had time to meet us. We met with Shimon Peres, who was making a toast for peace when the lights went out. Moshe Dayan served us tea and crumpets at his house, which looked like an archaeological museum, the backyard filled with ruins, pillars and statuary. We went to the Golan Heights and flew in Israeli helicopters to the West Bank of the Jordan River to inspect the status of the Israeli Army and discuss the interesting personnel management problems inherent to an army where a high percentage of the soldiers are Orthodox Jews.

My biggest thrill was meeting a true heroine, Golda Meir. When I commented on the stress of living in a state of red alert, she nodded and said with wonderful sangfroid, "We live in a tough neighborhood." I discovered that she had a real soft spot for Denver, having attended high school there in 1913–14. Years later I learned that the house she had lived in during that time was due to be razed. Many community leaders didn't care about saving it because it wasn't fancy, but I said, "You'll have to kill me before you touch one brick." Today that house is part of the Metro State College campus.

At a dinner in Tel Aviv, some of the congressmen were talking about going "trawling." I knew the term had something to do with fishing, but I couldn't figure out how and why they would do it after dinner. Late that night I was awakened by pounding on the wall of my hotel room, coming from the room next door occupied by a Southern congressman. I realized that trawling had nothing to do with fish. I wanted to get some sleep, so I called his room and asked him to please pull his bed away from the wall. He did, but at breakfast the next morning, I learned I had violated an unwritten, ironclad rule of codels: Hear no exploits, see no exploits, mention no exploits. This colleague later sat next to me on the plane and told me a sob story about one of his children being in trouble with the law and his wife asking him to cancel the Mideast trip to help the family get through the crisis. But he was looking for sympathy in the wrong corner. I told him that his wife was right and he should have stayed home—violation of the rule that one always sides with a colleague. I just never learned.

At that time, it was impossible to travel from Israel to Egypt with an Israeli stamp on your passport, so we had to change our papers in Cyprus. The Spanish Embassy handled the logistics for our visit because the United States had no embassy in Egypt. When we arrived in Cairo, the city was blacked out, and we were warned not to walk about unaccompanied. American-made tanks that had been captured in Israel were sitting in city parks, plastered with anti-American slogans. The Israelis were encamped across the Suez Canal at Kilometer 101, but the fighting had stopped, and officials on both sides were trying to negotiate a truce. We visited the city of Port Said, seeing

Dallas, Texas, 1947.
Watch out, John Wayne!

At the Plymouth
Congregational Church in
Des Moines, Iowa, 1962.
Does Jim know what he is
getting into?

A photo from Jim's campaign for Colorado legislature, 1970. Look where that political path led!

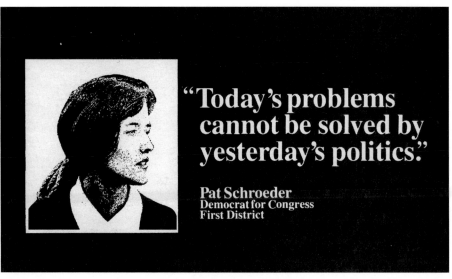

"Today's problems cannot be solved by yesterday's politics."

Pat Schroeder
Democrat for Congress
First District

Some of my first campaign literature — not exactly high style: black and white and cost one cent apiece.

Sargent Shriver appeared
at a campaign event
for me in 1972.

The family, 1975. They refused to dress up. So, if you can't fight them,
join them. (Obviously, we didn't use the photo in the campaign.)

Yes—they dressed up! Finally a
usable family photo!

From left to right: Congressman Gillis Long (Louisiana), me, Speaker Carl
Albert (Oklahoma), Jack Brooks (Texas), Tip O'Neill (Massachusetts). This is a
breakfast that Brooks gave for each freshman class—with meat he killed such as
quail or deer. Choke! Once I sat next to him on a plane and he started talking
about how eagle tasted just like swan. He was trying to jerk my leash. I had my
photo with an eagle in my briefcase, whipped it out and said, "You shouldn't say
that to people who have pet eagles!" It really set him back.

Denver Chamber of Commerce breakfast, 1975. Jamie signals she knows the game.

Jamie and Scott in D.C. with their beloved frog mirror. You never know what children will bond with.

First day of school, 1975.

St. Patrick's Day in Denver. Third from left: Dale Tooley, Denver district attorney; Mark Hogan, lieutenant governor of Colorado; Denver Mayor Bill McNichols, two radio/TV personalities, then me. Lighten up, gang!

A Denver St. Patrick's Day Parade with a mountain man military escort.

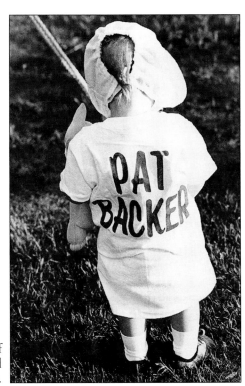

This came from a picnic rally of a pint-sized backer. We loved backers of all sizes.

Child care photo for campaign. Sometimes I wish five-year-olds could vote!

The 1974 campaign. I wish I could do computer enhancement of my outfit. What was I thinking?

Speaker Carl Albert after my swearing-in in 1973. A nice man from Bugtussle, Oklahoma.

At a bill signing in the White House Rose Garden, June 1976. Are we having fun yet?

At a charity event. Members of Congress participated, and people paid money to see us make fools of ourselves. No one needs a personal trainer more than I do.

When the Ringling Brothers Circus came to D.C., politicians were often invited to ride the elephants. It was one of the few things about Washingtion that got my kids excited, so I did it. Richard Nixon also rode one, but he wore a suit. How do those showgirls do it in opera hose?

In my office during
the early years.

Celebrating the House's first women pages. With Margaret Heckler, Leonor
Sullivan, Patsy Mink, Martha Griffiths, and Lindy Boggs in 1973–4.

Top row from left: Olympia Snowe, Geraldine Ferraro, Millicent Fenwick, Shirley Chisholm, Lindy Boggs. Bottom row from left: me, Doug Fraser (UAW), Margaret Heckler, Mary Rose Oakar, Barbara Mikulski. As a group, we were fearless and plowed into every issue possible.

With Mikulski, Boggs, Heckler (and four male colleagues). We were never afraid to laugh.

Congresswomen in China, 1975. Right row, from top: Mink, Miner, Collins, Heckler, Fenwick, Abzug. Left row, from top: me, Burke, Spellman, Holtzman. It was January and International Women's Year. Travel tip: January is *not* China's best month!

Mo Udall campaigned for me, and I was a Udall delegate to the '76 convention. He was a one-eyed, basketball-playing Mormon from Arizona with a great sense of humor.

At Lowrey base, Denver. I always envied the stature, composure, and majestic quietness of Native Americans. I looked frantic by comparison.

Barbara Jordan (Texas) during a 1976 Denver campaign rally. Listening to her magnificent voice, I felt that I had God on my side.

The Schroeder family overdresses for a visit to the Carter White House. Mom was out of town and the dress code collapsed.

A photo op with President Carter on Capitol Hill. Well, I guess I can no longer complain about how the kids dressed when they met the president!

At a White House meeting in the Cabinet Room during the Carter administration. We did not appreciate his openness at the time, but we sure did later on.

The backs of Tip O'Neill (Massachusetts), Tom Foley (Washington), Jim Wright (Texas), and Bill Alexander (Arkansas). This is the weekly Democratic Whip meeting—held in the morning on the third floor of the Capitol. This is where we got our marching orders. Actually, it was like trying to get a group of cats to drill together.

Congressman Charles Wilson (California), who headed a postal subcommittee I was on. I wonder why we looked so glum?

With Bill Gray (Pennsylvania) and Tip O'Neill. What a wonderful
human being Tip was. His heart was the size of a washtub.

Mo Udall, Tip O'Neill,
Mickey Leland (Texas).
Who says there are no
good folks in politics?

Lindy Boggs, Peggy Heckler, me.
Retiring the gavel to Peggy,
founder of the Congressional
Women's Caucus, in 1978. Is this
how the guys do it?

firsthand the death and destruction caused by U.S.-made fragmentation bombs. We met with the Egyptian Second Army troops on the east bank of the Suez. The commander of the Egyptian military gave a briefing that went on and on and on for hours. Members of our delegation were passing around a note, as if it were junior high math class, stifling laughter after they read it. The note had been written by Charles Melvin "Mel" Price (Democrat from Illinois), who later became chairman of the Armed Services Committee. It read, "If the Egyptians gave this briefing to the Israelis, they'd surrender."

President Anwar el-Sadat was staying outside Cairo in his summer palace, which looked as if it was decorated with furnishings that fell off the royal family's truck as it fled and were not maintained. There were red velvet chairs pulled over the worn parts of the rugs where the nap had died. Mrs. Sadat was not present, as she was going to hospitals to visit children who'd had shrapnel from American-made Israeli bombs surgically removed from their bodies.

The speaker and members of the Egyptian parliament were present, but Sadat asked them to leave the room. Then he laid out his vision for a peaceful coexistence with Israel that later became his trademark. "We've got to find a way to lower these barriers of hate," he said, but he was afraid to say it in front of his own people. Every time he went to pray at the mosque, he knew he could be shot. After our meeting, we wondered: Is this the new peacemaker, or is it that he's lost half his land and wants it back, especially the part with oil under it? A photograph of me with Sadat appeared on the front page of the Cairo newspaper. I didn't realize it would become a memento mori.

Although the American media had followed and photographed our group for ten days, the footage that was picked up for the network evening news showed several of us riding camels, the one "tourist" event of the entire trip, sponsored by our Egyptian hosts. A Denver newspaper, one that had endorsed me the year before, carried a prominent article attacking the trip because of the amount of jet fuel being used by the Air Force 707 to support our frivolous camel rides. Another local paper highlighted my view that the United States should proceed with "caution" and listen to Sadat's vision for peace. This touched off an immediate adverse reaction from my Jewish supporters. (Their furor was inflamed by the fact that Bill Armstrong, the other freshman congressman from Colorado who was on the trip, was shown in a photograph with Golda Meir while they ran one of me with Sadat. I had to repeat over and over, "I don't pick the pictures.") But in the aftermath of that trip, our government started meeting with Sadat and gave diplomatic recognition to Egypt. Our trip was the first step toward the historic meeting of Israeli Prime Minister Menachem Begin and Sadat in 1979 and the peace process we all pray is still progressing in that troubled area.

Being on Armed Services, I had the opportunity to meet world leaders everywhere. Many, like the Contras in Nicaragua, could not charm me, no matter what they said or did. Other cases were not so black or white. I was terribly conflicted about Prime Minister Benazir Bhutto of Pakistan. I wanted to support her because of her historic role: an Islamic woman in an arranged marriage taking her impoverished nation from military rule to democracy. But the issue of her country ignoring nuclear proliferation prevented me from extending my full support, as did growing allegations about using her power for personal gain, and a fortune possibly amassed from graft. The investigation into these charges, which Bhutto attacks as political persecution, is ongoing.

One of the fascinating things about being in Congress is the parade of world leaders, kings and queens, sports figures, movie stars and TV personalities who pass through. We live in such a tabloid culture that it's easy to trade on even peripheral exposure to famous people. I could lean into a party crowd and whisper conspiratorially, "You know, King Hussein doesn't wear undershirts" — instantly, I'd become very popular, and who could prove me wrong? Feeding the hunger for such trivia can be addictive.

But I am *very* uncomfortable with this celebrity fixation. I think it's great that Whoopi Goldberg, Glenn Close, Elizabeth Taylor and Barbra Streisand take time out from their careers to engage in the public debate on (respectively) abortion rights, prison reform, AIDS, and *anything*. There's often resentment about rich, famous, unelected celebrities putting forth their own agendas because they can afford to fly in, first class, and command an audience. But anyone who takes on these causes thinking it will enhance her career is crazy. It's risky business because they're not in control, there's no script, and there could be financial repercussions if fans disapprove. I found every one of them caring, concerned and a little shy, outside their normal stomping ground. I'd be a bit starstruck, meeting someone I'd only seen larger-than-life on a screen, but they were vulnerable, looking to me for direction in this new forum. I am glad they took their citizenship duties seriously. This is a country where you can ignore such responsibilities if you want, and many do.

The kings and queens and CEOs were different. They were there as part of their job description, leading a country or a company. They either needed government help or wanted government out of the way. Kings and queens are always the best at these public events. They've been trained since infancy for these roles, and the public face never cracks. I always wondered what they really thought, really wanted, or really cared about. Did they even know?

When I first came to Congress, committee chairmen were demigods. Younger representatives were to wait their turn, be quiet, and hope to outlive the opposition. If they made it to a committee chairmanship, they were there for life. But in 1974, the first post-Watergate group of representatives arrived in Congress ready for reform. They had the audacity to summon the chairman of every committee, to appear in front of their class asking for a report about their goals for each committee. The Democratic Caucus, under pressure from these freshman firebrands, changed the rules about committee chairmanship, making it mandatory that all chairs be elected by a majority of the party. The voting was by secret ballot at the beginning of each term, effective immediately. A chairmanship was no longer an honor in perpetuity. It was the end of seniority's iron rule.

When Hébert realized what was imminent, he tried a crash course in charm, but it was too late. My painful two years of sparring with him helped brand him as the autocrat he was, and other members joined the freshmen to remove him. (He was replaced by Mel Price.) Ron Dellums and I each got our own seat in the meeting room, and in 1992, Ron became full chairman of the Armed Services Committee. I'm sure that Hébert, who died in 1979, was spinning in his grave.

I seemed to run over part of the sacred congressional

culture on a daily basis. I was oblivious to the rules and the culture. Congressman Gillespie V. "Sonny" Montgomery of Mississippi was a classic Southern gentleman, a bachelor and a "boll weevil" (the endearing term for conservative southern Democrats, as "gypsy moth" is used to describe progressive northern Republicans). I was probably the most radical person he'd ever met, but he'd always been pleasant to me. Shortly after I arrived in Washington, he invited me to be a guest speaker at the Thursday morning congressional prayer breakfast, perhaps thinking it would tame me. Proud of my active membership in the Congregational Church, I launched into a freewheeling soliloquy, proposing a new eleventh commandment for Congress: "Thou shalt not bullshit thy colleagues." I described my shock at the number of times a congressman called a colleague a "distinguished gentleman" to his face and ten minutes later called him an SOB behind his back. I quoted Dr. Martin Luther King Jr. that we either live together as brothers and sisters or perish as fools. Then I read some poetry by Dory Previn about relating honestly to each other. I was quite pleased with myself for being so insightful. But Sonny Montgomery was white as a sheet. It seemed that the prayer group had only wanted me to read some polite Bible verses and sit down. A few of the conservative faction went to the press gallery and said I had violated the sensibilities of every member present by swearing at the prayer breakfast. I called Congressman Andrew Young (Democrat from Georgia), a fellow freshman and an ordained minister in my church, who told the press that Congregationalists are irrepressible and tend to act like that.

About ten years later my own minister in Denver witnessed the consequences of having my big mouth in his flock. The Reverend Stuart Haskins called me from a Colorado Council of Churches meeting where a resolution to censure me had been proposed. The group making this proposal had come to Washington a few months before to discuss a plan to feed and clothe the people in the refugee camps of southeast Asia. I supported their plan but not their insistence that the refugees must first be baptized to receive aid.

"This is where I leave you," I told the proselytizers in my office. "I do not see our role there as missionaries."

"You're a secular humanist," they insisted. "How can you call yourself a Christian?"

I thought their proviso constituted religious coercion and tried to change their minds, but they were intractable. After a good deal of argument, they proposed that we pray together so I would come to my senses. I refused, explaining that I did not mix my personal and public lives, and certainly did not pray on command. They went berserk: No one else had refused to pray. Their parting words were not exactly Christian, and now they were going to get even with a censure resolution. That's when my pastor came through. The world is full of people who say, "Why can't you just go along this once?" but when Stuart heard about my adventure with the church ladies, he said, "Good for you, and I'll handle it." He did: The resolution never went anywhere.

Sometimes I got to outwit the poobahs. Every spring, Washington has a Cherry Blossom Festival, where each state is represented by a "princess." The Colorado State Society, a group of expatriate Coloradans living in Washington, sponsored our state's princess and rotated the responsibility for her selection among the various congressional offices. It was very nepotistic—a lot of them simply named their own daughters. In 1979, having exhausted the rest of the delegation, they let me have a turn. I selected a bright, energetic young woman named Jo Zirkelbach, who had been a sitter for my children. I was expecting to escort her to the reception on Capitol Hill, but there was a slight problem: The rules of the Cherry Blossom Festival Society stipulated that only men could serve as escorts. I was encouraged to designate my husband or a suitable (i.e., male) member of the Colorado delegation to replace me. Instead I went to a costume store and bought an Easter bunny suit—there may have been a prohibition against escorts wearing dresses, but there was nothing in the rule book about cottontails. Jo loved the idea and entered the grand state procession of princesses with a giant rabbit on her arm. The Colorado Society never let me have another turn at selecting the princess, but the rabbit story wasn't over yet.

Easter of 1979 the Armed Services Committee was going to China to learn about the Chinese military after the border war it had with Vietnam. It was actually my second trip: All the women in Congress had gone to Beijing three years earlier to celebrate the Year of the Woman. Speaking with Americans living there, I learned it was hard for them to keep holiday traditions for their children. Now, being the proud owner of a rabbit suit, I packed it in my suitcase. The American mission was led by Leonard Woodcock, former head of the United Auto Workers, who'd been appointed ambassador to China by President Jimmy Carter. He had planned an egg hunt at his home on Easter Sunday and told me to be sure to bring the suit. I was mobbed by little American ankle-biters thrilled to see their first Easter bunny. It was a Kodak moment for expatriate parents.

A week later when our returning military plane touched down at Andrews Air Force base outside Washington, one of the crew members came back and said the press corps had gathered where we were deplaning, wanting to see my bunny suit. Apparently when the story was reported in the United States, I was said to have traveled all over China dressed as a rabbit, and editorial writers were raging about such juvenile behavior. I tried to set the record straight, but no one in the press would have it. They knew I was lying. Finally I gave up. I issued a statement that Congress would be a better place if more members wore rabbit suits instead of power suits and donated the infamous costume to the Denver Children's Museum.

———————————

Everything is magnified in public life, so the actions and reactions of politicians can reverberate, disastrously. One morning in 1986 Barney Frank called in a panic, asking me to contact the Speaker, Tip O'Neill, immediately. He feared that the *Washington Post* would be reviewing a book written by Robert Bauman, who had been a vicious gay-basher while he was a Republican congressman but, once out of public office, admitted he was himself gay. Bauman didn't stop at being a hypocritical snake. Filled with latter-day righteous indignation, he had decided to set the record straight, so to speak, and "out" other homosexuals, including Barney. Since Barney and the Speaker were both from Massachusetts, the press was likely to ask for Tip's reaction, and his response would be critical.

I don't know what I thought the Speaker's response would be, but I was unprepared for the intensity of his words. "I just can't figure out those queers," he said. "I hear they're all over Congress. Why would anyone want to be a queer?" As I stared in disbelief, I realized I did not have the gravitas to head off this disaster, and I fled to find his press reps, retelling the story and screaming "Damage control!"

Fortunately, the *Post* review of the book did not mention Barney, and we had a little more time for the reeducation of Tip O'Neill. There was no more loving person on the planet, but he came from a generation of men that did not discuss homosexuality and grew up talking about being "happy and gay." I'm not even sure he knew that "queer" was a prejudicial, narrow-minded and politically incorrect term. I don't think he meant it to be insulting, any more than another person of his generation who might use the word "colored" or "Negro" rather than "black" or "African-American." I don't think his remark was meant to be hurtful. When Barney disclosed his sexual orientation himself, the Speaker was gracious with a statement of support. Privately, he told me that he was disappointed because he thought Barney had a chance to be the first Jewish Speaker of the House, an opportunity that might now be compromised.

Unwittingly, I got in trouble with a gay constituency myself. When I have a lot of speaking engagements back-to-back, I'd love to give each group a completely original, well thought-out discourse, but I tend to go on automatic pilot: Push a button and the speech pours out. One evening I had four tightly scheduled events, starting with the Gertrude Stein Democratic Club of Washington, a gay and lesbian group. I was giving my regular pep talk about the damage done during the Reagan administration as a clarion call to vote. "For years," I said, "I've felt like the little Dutch boy with his finger in the dike." Throughout the room, I could hear the whispering and tittering getting louder and louder, and finally my brain processed my huge gaffe. I don't think I could have blushed because there was no blood flowing. My heart stopped. I looked to the back of the room to see my husband turning whiter every second and backing out the door. I finished my speech—I think I would have been clocked at three-hundred words per minute—and made an excuse about hurrying on to other events.

When I got to the car, I was almost physically ill. A few articles about my insensitivity appeared in the gay press, and naturally word of my faux pas reached my congressional colleagues. Representative Dave Martin (Republican from New York) was the ranking member on the military subcommittee I chaired and a great prankster. When he heard about the incident, he had a painting made of a Dutch boy with his finger in a dike. He even went to the trouble of printing stationery with the group's letterhead at the top and sent a letter on it saying please accept the group's thanks for the speech, and that everyone understood I didn't mean it the way the press portrayed it. Naively (some would say idiotically) I thought the praise was genuine and within an hour after I received it I sent a flowery thank-you note for the kind words. Dave called finally because I hadn't responded to his joke. I discovered I'd done it again. Thank goodness my friends in the gay and lesbian community have large hearts, great patience and a wonderful sense of humor.

3

Change Sparring Partners and Dance

O ne constant about Washington is: The players keep changing. But I never expected that the change during my first term in Congress would mean the resignation and near-impeachment of a president. During the Watergate era, everybody in the capital ran out in their bathrobes each morning to get the papers. We were obsessed with the latest minutiae of the drama. When the House Judiciary Committee started listening to the infamous Oval Office tapes, the members would emerge ashen-faced from the hearing room one by one (there were only so many headsets available). Barbara Jordan and Liz Holtzman were both on the Judiciary Committee and seemed particularly shaken: What if you were a "freshman" and voted to impeach the president of the United States?

Nixon had always been "Tricky Dick," the man who

had defeated fellow Californian Helen Gahagan Douglas for Congress in possibly the ugliest campaign in history. I had a postcard of him fishing with President Eisenhower, wearing wing-tipped shoes—we got the feeling that he could not relax. But once we could hear the venom and irrationality of his private personality, we started whispering among ourselves about the fact that this man still had a finger on the proverbial button.

The impeachment tom-toms were beating when the Armed Services Committee made its trip to the Middle East. The plane sat waiting on the ground at Andrews Air Force Base for several hours while most of the other committee members were summoned to a meeting at the White House. Even the staunchest Republicans arrived at the plane rattled. Nixon had entered the Oval Office with an American flag pin upside down on his lapel, and he was showing evidence of the cornered rat syndrome. "I want people to get off my back," he said. "I'm not going to take it anymore." He pointed to the hot phone. "Do you realize," he asked the startled congressmen, "that all I have to do is pick up that phone, and we could be at nuclear war?" I worried about that until I asked a CIA guy if it was true. "Of course it has to be connected," he told me.

The Denver Bar Association asked me to give a speech on the legal grounds for impeachment. It was scary to be there, a very, very junior politician, setting out the thirty-two different counts that the Judiciary Committee was considering. I wasn't sure how these much more experienced lawyers would react, and it was one of the few times I followed a prepared text. Everybody in the audience was grim-faced and took my comments with the solemnity befitting the occasion, intuiting that this was no time for political gamesmanship. In Washington my office was equipped with a WATS line, and I let some of the people organizing for impeachment come in to make phone calls after hours. One day a stranger came up to me in Dulles Airport, said, "We have your phones tapped," and walked away.

The resignation came so quickly that the joke going around town was that Nixon never had time to get his deck shoes off the yacht. (The president still had a yacht then, called *Sequoia*. Jimmy Carter sold it.) I had a brilliant idea the day Nixon left the White House lawn in a helicopter, with that famous salute and fake smile. Members of Congress are permitted to purchase an American flag and give it to one of the pages, who dates it and flies it above the Capitol. I thought: *This is the day*. I bought a whole bunch of flags and had each of them hoisted onto the Capitol flagpole for a few minutes. For years afterward, I had a pile ready to go any time I was asked to donate a souvenir for a charity auction.

Gerald Ford was a decent fellow—he got up and toasted his own muffin in the morning, so how bad could he be?—but he inherited the detritus of Watergate and never really had a chance. I knew him as the House minority leader when I arrived in Congress. He was very athletic, but the press portrayed him as a klutz, running the tapes of him tripping over and over. One of my college sorority sisters was Betty Ford's niece. During the '76 campaign, she wrote and asked, "Should we come to Washington and visit now, or should we wait until after the election?" I said, "Come now," pretty sure there would be no "after."

But in a relatively short period of time, Betty Ford *did* things. It would be difficult to say which of her two major projects had more lasting and profound results: the California clinic to treat substance abuse that she founded after affirming her own drug habit, acquired while being treated by the best doctors in the country; or her testimony about breast cancer research after revealing her own mastectomy. This was revolutionary stuff. Twenty years ago a woman diagnosed with breast cancer did not talk about it, except in a whisper to her closest friends. And pharmaceutical companies were practically complicit in prescription drug abuse, conveying in their medical journal advertising the suggestion that women should live in a pink fog. They advocated that pills be shoved at any woman who appeared nervous or acted out. Open discussion of these issues was as limited and haphazard as discussion of family violence is today. The O. J. Simpson trial may have fast-forwarded public awareness of domestic abuse, but many women are still prevented from seeking help by misplaced shame and humiliation, and that was the prevalent attitude about drug abuse and "the big C" in the early seventies.

While Betty Ford ushered in a more free and open discussion, there was still no action on women's health issues. In the '70s, nobody knew much about breast cancer unless she had it. Then, almost overnight, everybody knew somebody who had it. When Betty Ford started talking about the disease, about the need for prevention and early detection and funding for treatment options, I thought: *This is the president's wife — now everyone will listen.* But it wasn't so. Policy-makers forgot as soon as they were confronted with funding choices. I began meeting with breast cancer survivors and women's health-care providers. We realized we can spend the rest of our lives looking for celebrities to come forward and make news on this subject, or we can organize to make our representatives see that their support for legislative action translates to votes in their districts. That was the beginning of the National Breast Cancer Coalition, founded in 1991. Three times, through our lobbying efforts, we got mammograms included in Medicare coverage. Each time that the Ways and Means Committee returned from conference with its counterpart from the Senate, the provision was gone, as if it was written in disappearing ink. Congress funds what it fears, and our mostly male Congress didn't fear breast cancer. They didn't think of their wives, mothers, daughters and sisters while casting their votes. Our job was to make them remember or know that we would forget to vote for them in November. The going got tough, so the tough got going!

The rest is history. The Breast Cancer Coalition is now a model for women all over the world to emulate.

In 1976 I supported Congressman Morris Udall (Democrat from Arizona) for president. He was the head of our region—our shepherd. I loved Mo's humor—his memoirs were called *Too Funny to Be President*. When I first arrived in Washington, he told me the difference between a cactus and a caucus: The cactus has its pricks on the outside. So Jimmy Carter was not my first choice, but when he won the election, I was thrilled that a member of my own party was president after a Republican epoch. I was fascinated by the New Georgians in the White House. The Carter style was foreign to me—out west back then, we were suspicious of people who discussed their religious beliefs openly—but the Carters were so reachable and real, so earnest and affable. One weekend before the election, I saw the Carters at the National Zoo. It wasn't a prearranged photo op, but a genuine family outing, and I thought: *I'm going to like him.* I loved the fact that they let Amy have a treehouse and that Rosalynn didn't buy a new dress for the inaugural.

I worked with President Carter on an issue in my own state that I came to think of as the damn dams. Colorado was slated to get millions of dollars in funding to build three dams, but the truth was, we didn't need them. We already had huge farm surpluses, and all the dams would do was make some unnecessary arid land arable, in the process increasing the salinity of the soil and doing all sorts of other environmental damage. We also would have been in violation of our treaty with Mexico on the quality of river-water runoff. Jimmy Carter tried to explain this situation in a western summit conference, but the local papers saw only that their state was being denied money. I wrote op-ed pieces about water recycling until I could spout the statistics in my sleep, but my opponent in my reelection campaign of 1980 chose to make me sound like an idiot. ("She doesn't want the dams, and wants you to drink garbage.")

Neither Carter's staff nor his extended family served him very well. There were regular imbroglios from the "Georgia Mafia": Hamilton Jordan saying unpleasant things about women's breasts, Billy Carter saying almost anything. Carter's staff pissed off Tip O'Neill pretty fast, giving the impression that they thought of Tip as that old dinosaur. They were experts at offending people who should have been their allies.

Then came the Iran hostage crisis. Every newscast opened with "Day__: America held Hostage." The voters pinned the blame on Carter, labeled him a wimp and sent him back to Georgia. He has gone on, without the staff, to be the best ex-president I've seen.

Then came Ronald Reagan. No one knows how many minks gave their lives for Ronald Reagan's inauguration. Big black cars and dark brown furs are the predominant images in my memory when I think of the 1981 Reagan invasion of Washington. I knew how out of place I was going to be when a prosperous-looking woman came up to me at one of the swish inaugural balls and asked, "Whose dress is that?" Ignorant of designers, I answered, "Mine." It would be a very long eight years.

The Reagan years were the era of the ladies who lunch, of women as geishas. To be a player, a man needed a trophy wife (the paradigm being Georgette Mosbacher or Ariana Huffington). A standard line around town was that you knew how much lettuce a guy had by the type of tomato he was with. The Style section of the *Washington Post* ran frequent stories about Nancy Reagan's wealthy friends visiting Washington and keeping their jewels in the hotel safe. It was as if the Windsors had been elected to office. Everybody was buying red dresses, and not off the local rack; the "right" clothes came from designer boutiques. After Rosalynn Carter making her own clothes, it was enough to give you the bends. Washington became a movie set, and women were allowed only minor supporting roles.

It was a devastating period for serious policy-making about issues of concern to women. The new women's issues were: Where is your diamond insured? and Who is your decorator? The Equal Rights Amendment died. I remember going to the White House with a gold ERA pin on my lapel and being asked to take it off. "Don't we have free speech here anymore?" I asked one of the staff. "The president believes in little 'e,' little 'r,' little 'a,'" I was told. What did that mean?

The message from the Reagan administration was: "We don't deal with women who demonstrate, so lower your voice and put on some pearls." This had the effect of quashing much public debate. Only when NOW was out on the street making noise would the president summon a few "ladies" to the Oval Office, handpicked by the White House for a photo op. But even the female "leaders" who put on their finest suits, thinking they'd meet him on his own terms, still didn't get anywhere with him. No matter what the pretense for a meeting, any encounter with President Reagan was nothing more than a "meet and greet," where he told stories about his movie career. Nobody was willing to interrupt the leader of the free world and tell him to focus, so the meeting would be over and the "issues" never discussed. Reagan was said to be a "generalist," a "big-picture guy." And he could charm a snake. The deficit was soaring, and people were beginning to realize he had talked them into a hot-fudge-sundae diet that wasn't working. He was actually starting to get into trouble when he was shot in 1981 outside the Washington Hilton. Criticism stopped abruptly, and you know the rest of the story.

The Reagan presidency was a parade of wonderful visuals. Once elected, he never met with the Women's Caucus, even though we requested meetings repeatedly and even though he granted meetings to the Black and Hispanic Caucuses. Mrs. Reagan agreed to one luncheon with us, but there were constant calls from her office dictating the terms of her appearance: No substantive issues were to be discussed. I considered sending her staff a copy of the First Amendment but decided it would be counterproductive.

I was seated next to her at the luncheon and could find absolutely nothing to say that was not considered verboten. (The devil in me wanted to ask, "How are the kids?" but I decided that would be tacky.) The mood of the luncheon was stiff and cold, and when the caucus met again we had bipartisan agreement that any further attempt to engage Mrs. Reagan would be a massive waste of time. So no elected female leaders in either party got to discuss women's equity with the president or the First Lady for eight years.

I had only one personal phone call from Ronald Reagan the whole time I was in Congress. He had made some comment against the Denver Broncos, favoring their opponents in the big pre–Super Bowl hype, so I sent him a pair of Bronco boxer shorts with a note that said, "You shouldn't pick favorites, and I hope you'll wear these." And he called me to say thank you. That was the level on which the Great Communicator was willing to communicate—sports and movies, but not policy. I certainly never heard from him regarding what became his lasting epithet. During the 1984 campaign, Democrats were desperate to find some sound bite describing Reagan's reign. One morning I was scrambling eggs in a Teflon pan for my kids and it suddenly occurred to me: *That's what's wrong—this man is the Teflon president. Nothing he does sticks to him.* I went to the House floor and gave a one-minute speech invoking that phrase. A lot of the network news programs carried my speech. I think the term resonates because it was one of the few political metaphors that wasn't a sports analogy.

Although I never heard from Reagan or his team about it, I did get a letter from the lawyers at DuPont, the manufacturer of Teflon, threatening to sue me for trademark infringement. But the real surprise was the response of other politicians. Instead of reacting with outrage and a demand to scrape off Reagan's Teflon coating, they mostly asked: How do we get the same protection? The Teflon kept working: George Bush, Reagan's lieutenant, spent the next four years in the White House.

When Bush won the Republican nomination for president at the 1988 convention in New Orleans, I was covering the event with Pat Buchanan for *Good Morning America.* I really had nothing to do, like a wallflower at a hookers' ball, so I spent most of the time wandering around the convention floor. People would come up to me and say, "I know your face—can I have my picture taken with you?" Then, halfway through the snapping of the lens, they'd realize who I was. "Destroy the film" ran through their heads.

I don't know why Bush picked Dan Quayle as his running mate, whether he wanted somebody young or just wanted to look like a rocket scientist in comparison. What the two had in common was their trust funds—they were both members of what I call the lucky sperm club. They were always giving speeches about pulling yourself up by your bootstraps, which is easier when the boots are Guccis—that good leather doesn't snap so easily.

Quayle would fight tooth and nail, saying he was middle-class. (Every American thinks he's middle class, except William F. Buckley Jr.) But I knew that his family connections had kept him out of Vietnam. My staff had put together a list of the chicken hawks in Congress, which I'd never used for political purposes—I felt it would have a lot more credibility if it came from a man who had served in the war. The only war I served in was the war on poverty. But I thought it was time to mention his chicken hawk status on *GMA* when Bush announced his running mate. Buchanan could hardly muster a protest—he never served in Vietnam either. Suddenly I became very busy in New Orleans.

When Bush took office, we Democrats were certain

things would be different. He had a progressive record as a congressman—like a "gypsy moth" out of Texas, although he served for only one term. (Bush was renting a post office box in Texas in order to keep his claim to it as a home state. His roots were in Connecticut, but still it was a real stretch to see him living anywhere but Washington, after his years as head of the CIA, chairman of the Republican Party and ambassador to China.) Barbara Bush was certainly more approachable than Nancy Reagan and supported wonderful projects concerning disadvantaged women and literacy. When Bush gave the speech about a "kinder, gentler" America, I think he meant it. If he did, he soon lost his will to put it into action. We thought he had an agenda, but when I look back on his four years, I can't figure out what it was: He kept talking about his "vision" thing.

Both Reagan and Bush seemed terrified of women's issues. They appointed some women to Cabinet positions and deflected questions about women's legislation by pointing to them. As president, Bush vetoed the Family Medical Leave Act that he had promised to support when he was campaigning. I was crushed.

Next he put another dagger in my heart with his veto of the Women's Health Equity Act. Every year Congress allots millions of tax dollars to the National Institutes of Health for the best medical research on the planet. In the mid-1980s, I was reading the results of these NIH-funded studies and realized that they always referred to men eating fish, men drinking coffee, men taking aspirin, men jogging, men aging. . . . I wondered: *Does "men" mean "men and women"?* I was sure it must. Why would NIH ignore half the nation's taxpayers?

I talked to my congressional colleagues Olympia Snowe and Henry Waxman, and we jointly asked for the General Accounting Office to give us a profile of health-study participants. To our collective dismay, we discovered that "men" meant "men." NIH had even conducted its breast cancer studies on men. There was no division or center for obstetrics or gynecology, but there was one for urology. The government's primary allocator of medical-research dollars was in such total fear of females that even the lab rats were male.

The way these decisions were made is NIH finds doctors who are "leading experts" doing "premier research" and puts them on panels that receive requests for future research. Guess who was sitting at those tables? Men. They weren't interested in our concerns about women, arguing that such consideration was popularizing or politicizing pure research, making it lesser science.

Armed with the GAO report, we went to Congresswoman Connie Morella and Senator Barbara Mikulski, both of whom represent the Maryland district where NIH is located. Barbara, Connie and I met with the heads of the various institutes in Maryland. Their condescending attitude was stunning. They informed us that limiting studies to men was easier because any random group of men would all be in the same metabolic state. You see a random group of women might include some who were pregnant, some who were menopausal, some in different phases of their menstrual cycle. Men were simpler.

"But couldn't those different metabolic states necessitate different treatments?" we asked.

"Probably," they said. But if you didn't study it, no one knew.

NIH had just completed the largest study ever conducted on aging—with 75,000 men. The study did not address osteoporosis, bladder incontinence, menopause and other age-related issues of particular concern to women. We asked why women were not part of the study since women have a longer life expectancy than men and constitute a higher percentage of the aging population. NIH told us it was easier for research subjects to use the men's restrooms at their facilities.

This harmed women. The number-one killer of postmenopausal women is heart disease. When a man complains of symptoms associated with a heart attack, a red alert goes into effect in any hospital. But when a woman appears with identical symptoms, she is apt to receive casual treatment until her condition becomes critical. Doctors had never seen a study on heart problems that included women and often assumed they were immune to them. More

enlightened doctors were on their own to deduce from gov-
ernment-funded studies of men how to treat female
patients. Women's caregivers were like veterinarians, trying
to figure it out on their own.

Finally NIH agreed that its policy was wrong. I think
the people there figured we'd say we won something and
shut up and leave them alone. NIH agreed to include
women in future studies and promised to change their
regulations immediately. We were elated. But press stories
on medical research kept referring to "men." Several years
later we asked GAO to update the earlier survey. It turned
out that NIH did change the regulations but never
enforced them. The attitude was: "Politicians won't dic-
tate to us." We immediately went to work drafting the
Women's Health Equity Act, which mandated that NIH
establish an office of women's health to review every study
funded. It further stipulated mandatory inclusion of
women in studies if they are susceptible to the disease or
condition being researched. Certain gender-specific
research such as breast cancer, ovarian cancer and osteoporosis, previously ignored or seriously shortchanged by
NIH, would now receive direct funding.

The NIH scientists howled that Congress was politicizing and micromanaging them. But our goal was to know as
much about women's health as we know about men's health
by the year 2000, and we knew it was not their goal. The
tough had to get going again; they had blown their trust.

In September 1990, the acting director of NIH, William Raub, announced the creation of an Office of Research on Women's Health. I continued to take every speaking invitation I could get to organize for the Women's Health Equity Act. Women everywhere were enraged about the many years of neglect for their health concerns amid male hegemony. The Congresswomen's Caucus made the act the centerpiece of its legislative agenda, educating our colleagues one by one. We finally got the legislation through both the House and Senate in the same session, only to have George Bush veto it.

It was soon clear that the veto was a big political mistake. The president tried to deflect women's anger by appointing the first woman, Dr. Bernadine Healey, to head NIH, hiding behind her skirt when asked about the veto. It was the same old Reagan trick. When asked about a woman's policy, point to a female policy-maker you appointed. Dr. Healy, a past president of the American Heart Association and thus intimately acquainted with cardiac risk for women, met with our caucus and did include women in studies about aging, but women of childbearing age were still not addressed. Dr. Healy had to avoid the issue of abortion, which was such a hot potato for the Bush administration. I never knew whether she agreed with him philosophically or simply had all she could handle without tackling the most volatile health issue of the time. She opposed all research on fetal tissue and on RU-486, the "abortion pill."

RU-486 might have positively affected many other conditions, but we couldn't test it because the Bush administration feared its use for abortions. We tried to focus attention on the dichotomy of this position by calling a congressional hearing where Cybill Shepherd testified, as did a woman from Atlanta who had modeled with her. This woman was the wife of an "Eagle," meaning a major contributor to the Republican party. Her husband had an inoperable brain tumor, and doctors at Emory University said that RU-486 was his only hope of slowing the growth of the tumor. The Bush administration he had helped put in office denied his request. The hearing got great play, and the man finally got his RU-486. But we could not have a hearing and garner such publicity for every case. We needed a public policy permitting research and medical advances.

I think one of the major creators of the gender gap in the 1992 election was Bush's veto of the Family Leave and Women's Health Equity acts. Women were furious about Bush's action, and voted for Bill Clinton in big numbers.

Quite early in his presidency, Bill Clinton met with the Women's Caucus. It was our first official presidential meeting in twelve years. Usually, it's the president who's overscheduled and apt to dash out of any meeting after a few minutes, but he sat and talked with us for over two hours, until we were looking at our watches. We described our frustration about our long legislative agenda, dammed up by Bush's veto pen. He told us to start passing our bills again. We did—what a joy. He signed the Women's Health Equity Act and Family Medical Leave, lifted the outrageous restrictions on RU-486 and the gag rule prohibiting medical caregivers from discussing reproductive choices with women. Pens and photos from these bill-signings decorated my office. It was wonderful.

If I were Clinton, I'd be angry at my own party. Before he became president, he served as chairman of the Democratic Leadership Council—a centrist group. The buzz in the party was: "We have to nominate Clinton or we won't win. We've tried McGovern, we've tried Humphrey and Mondale, let's move to the middle of the road." Every other candidate was shut out. The strategy worked. But after Clinton was elected, the guys from the DLC were the ones who savaged him on issues like gays in the military, which exploded about fifteen minutes after he was sworn in. It didn't make any sense. They didn't even wait a week to wage war on their own guy.

People of every political stripe are always astonished at how engaging Clinton is, genuinely connecting with people, not looking over your shoulder to see if there's somebody more interesting or important. I've seen him at Christmas parties with hundreds of guests, and he stops for a photo op with every single one, never getting to eat or step onto the dance floor. When he leaves politics, he'll still be out there with the people, telling stories, exchanging ideas and cultivating an alert, intellectual mind. The thing I find amazing about him is that he really does his homework: You give him a book, and he gives it back— read *and* underlined.

One of the main things I hold against him is Dick Morris, who made himself sound like the U.S. cavalry riding over the hill to save his old friend in the 1996 campaign. Morris was the guy who came up with the concept of "triangulation": He decided that Clinton had to create as much distance between himself and Democrats as he did between himself and Republicans. This advice turned the president into an oscillating, wishy-washy namby-pamby, vulnerable to accusations of abandoning deeply held principles. Morris's insistence on cultivating the "Bubba" vote had Clinton talking about sowing green grass in the back of his pickup truck and other such silliness. The problem with Morris was that he was too far in the shadows to control. Many presidential appointees, such as Cabinet members, write a letter of resignation and give it to the president as soon as they're appointed. All he has to do is date it. I always thought that Clinton should have had such paperwork in his drawer from Morris.

Clinton has much better taste in wives than political advisers. We could not have designed a better advocate for "women's issues" than Hillary Rodham Clinton. Early in the first Clinton administration, she came to the House

office building and met with the Women's Caucus to discuss our concern that health care not get pushed to the
back of the agenda and that family planning not get conveniently overlooked or forsaken. Despite her historically
record-breaking involvement in policy-making, she
always had time for such meetings, never giving our
"female" concerns short shrift.

In hindsight, it seems that the Clintons were naive
about health-care reform. The polls may have said that people wanted reform, but the president needed more congressional support and a more effective counter-spin control to the Republicans' criticism. The lodge in Wyoming
full of experts telling him what the best plan was and why it
would work might very well have produced the best plan,
but to pass it he needed more input from Congress. I think
Clinton overreacted after that defeat. Now he needs to turn
off some of the input.

In the last election, the voter everyone was courting
was not Bubba but "the soccer mom." Watching TV
today, it is difficult to believe there was a time when
women's issues were ignored. Until ten years ago, campaigns were all about who's going to the moon and who's
got the most aircraft carriers. Female-friendly issues were
handled by the candidates' wives at tea parties mas-
querading as political meetings. Things began to change
when politicians were shown convincing evidence of a
"gender gap" in the 1988 election. Suddenly they wanted

to figure out how to talk to women voters. All of a sudden we started seeing candidates visiting day-care centers, looking as awkward in the presence of irrepressible toddlers as George Bush looked when he was introduced to the supermarket scanner. What next? Maybe in the year 2000 male politicians soliciting the female vote will wear "I feel your pain" high heels and empathetic pregnancy pillows in their trousers.

The antiapartheid cause was so dear to my heart that I was willing (even proud) to be jailed for my convictions. My abhorrence for apartheid dates back to my student government days, when we got the University of Minnesota to divest itself of investments with South African ties. We even funded ads asking students to boycott South African lobster tails and diamonds, not because we thought students were buying a lot of lobsters or diamonds, but we couldn't find any other South African products to boycott. South Africa was a police state where 16 percent of the population controlled everything and perpetuated racism.

At first supporters in the House could muster only one hundred votes condemning apartheid. Those who refused to come onboard argued that it was important to have American interests in South Africa because our country was the only forum for bringing blacks and whites together. They said our boycott would end up hurting the very people we were trying to help.

You can talk yourself into anything, especially if you have a moneyed interest. Congressmen who wouldn't sponser the antiapartheid legislation tried to make us sound irrational and overreactive. One of the lead sponsors on the Republican side was the Illinois Congressman John Anderson. Those were the days of moderate, independent Republicans (Paul N. "Pete" McCloskey of California was another) who were Lincolnesque: On market issues, they were conservative, but when it came to constitutional issues, they were right there fighting the good fight. Anderson had quite an independent streak, showing great courage in defying most of his party. That streak struck right out to his 1980 race for president on the Independent ticket, but he didn't have the kind of money of a Ross Perot. His campaign was fueled by direct mail. He was required, as any independent candidate would be, to process fifty different legal forms to get on the ballot in fifty states, a quantity of paperwork that would keep a firm of lawyers busy for a year. He didn't get on the ballot in many states, so many of his supporters were not able to vote for him. Nevertheless, he still got 6.6 percent of the vote.

President Reagan let the Afrikaners hide their miserable system behind him, giving them assurances that the boycott legislation would never go anywhere. He repeated the mantra that American companies were doing the only good work there, so why would we want to hurt them? It was embarrassing to see the leader of the free world wink at such inhumanity, but the winking only fired us up to push harder. In 1986 I joined many others in picketing the South African Embassy to protest against the twenty-seven-year internment of Nelson Mandela. The District of Columbia policemen had to enforce the law prohibiting protests outside an embassy. We were arrested, even though most of the arresting officers were in full support of our antiapartheid position. We were taken to a D.C. jail to be fingerprinted and photographed, but the entire incarceration lasted about an hour: The TransAfrica Group had organized the protest, and had attorneys in place to get us out. Only my mother, who was watching the TV news that night, was afraid that the children of a jailbird wouldn't get dinner.

There were more marches, more rallies, more picketing, more arrests, more grassroots organizing in the churches, and finally in 1986 the bill ordering government sanctions against South Africa passed in both the House and the Senate. The unraveling of apartheid had begun, and the velocity of change was stunning. Watching Nelson Mandela emerge from jail in 1990 and take the presidency seemed impossible. It never would have sold as the plot of a novel — too improbable.

Just before the historic election when, for the first

time, all citizens of South Africa could vote, the House sent a delegation there. It was led by Congressman John Lewis (Democrat from Georgia), who came out of the Southern Christian Leadership Conference and had a distinguished civil rights career going back to the days of Dr. Martin Luther King Jr. Lewis asked me to join him in achieving the trip's serious purpose. Chief Buthelezi led the Inkatha Freedom Party, supported by many Afrikaners. He refused to put his party on the ballot. Buthelezi had been the darling of President Reagan, and I think he was in shock that events had changed so rapidly. He was not buying into the electoral process and threatened to continue violent disruptions everywhere. Our mission was to change his mind.

In Johannesburg we boarded a van to visit Mandela at the African National Congress headquarters, but we had to turn back several times when snipers fired on us. Being shot at is a strange thing: Your first instinct should be: *Down, girl.* Instead you hear noises and think, *What's going on?* It takes awhile to compute that they're shooting at you. The American Embassy staffer who came to take notes on our meeting ended up spending the afternoon under a desk waiting for the gunfire to stop. Mandela finally arranged a meeting at a private home. Americans are accustomed to a type of civil rights dialogue that came out of the sixties, a lot of "We shall overcome" in the cadence of a prayer meeting. Mandela is very quiet and his words are calming—no bombast, no oratory. We kept expecting him to build to a crescendo, but he speaks in the cooler British tradition. We were in awe watching him navigate politically and emotionally after twenty-seven years in prison. Here was this incredible, forgiving pragmatist, embracing his captors.

In Capetown we had meetings with representatives of the different parties, trying to defuse some of the tension between the so-called Africans and the "coloreds" (who might be Asians or people of much lighter skin). There was actually a "pencil in the hair" test to determine race: Stick a pencil in someone's hair, and if the hair was curly and stiff enough to hold a pencil up, that person was considered African. We went to community centers in the colored neighborhoods to confront some of the backlash. And we attended Maundy Thursday services at Bishop Desmond Tutu's Episcopalian cathedral. He wore flaming scarlet robes and washed the feet of his congregation. Meeting with us afterward, he said he now knew there was a God because he finally got to vote for the first time in his life.

The city of Durban in Natal Province was an Afrikaner power base. The U.S. ambassador, Princeton Lyman, was scheduled to give a speech at an annual white-tie dinner of local movers and shakers. We went with him. His words were an eloquent exhortation to become part of a thrilling historic moment, but the audience sat stony-faced. They

were the backers of Buthelezi, who was the only black in
the room—an unholy alliance. After the speech, the five
of us in the American delegation clapped frantically while
the rest of the room remained frozen and silent. It was
haunting.

Our meetings with Buthelezi the following day were
tense. We tried to convey how history might portray him
if South Africa came so far in such a short period and then
blew up because he kept his party off the ballot, inciting
his followers to disrupt the elections. If looks could kill, I
would have been struck dead. It was bad enough for
Buthelezi to receive such a "blood on your hands" message from the men, but an audaciously outspoken woman
was too much. But somehow the message was absorbed.
After the ballots had been printed, Buthelezi agreed to put
his party on.

One of my greatest treasures from political life is a
framed copy of that historic ballot with the entry for the
Inkatha party taped on the bottom. After Mandela's victory, his extraordinary theme of reconciliation extended to
Buthelezi, who now holds a position in Mandela's administration.

Mandela's influence even extends to clearing the air of
the hubris attendant to foreign protocol. After his divorce
from Winnie Mandela, the president became involved
with Grace Machel, widow of the former president of
Mozambique. She will not marry because she lives most of

the time in Mozambique, carrying on the work she and her husband began. When Mandela and Machel travel together, the protocol offices go crazy. Nelson Mandela managed to puncture another bit of hypocrisy by introducing the political world's first official significant other.

4

A Pregnant Pause

The best preparation for infiltrating the boys' club of Congress was the boys' club of Harvard Law School. In 1961 there were fifteen women in my first-year class, and the five hundred men acted as if we constituted estrogen contamination. I was stunned when several of them insisted on changing their assigned seats in the lecture halls, as if mere proximity to women could be hazardous.

Elizabeth Dole was a year behind me. She was supposed to be in my class, but she couldn't decide if she wanted to be a lawyer, so Harvard held her spot for a year while she worked in the library. She lived across the street from me and several times forgot to put on her parking brakes so her car rolled into mine—Jim used to tease her about it when she became secretary of transportation. She's said that when she is reminiscing about law school and mentions some of the hateful behavior from the Harvard men, classmates that she actually remembers as friendly apologize for their own conduct. Maybe *none* of them thought women belonged there!

The dean certainly didn't. Erwin Griswold was a large white-haired man we called Cambridge Fats behind his back. He barked rather than talked—he would have been great in the military—and did everything by the book. There was a certain date in November to turn on the heat, and it didn't matter if Massachusetts was blizzarding in October, that was the day the heat got turned on. If people complained about the frigid temperature in the library, he would say, "Put on a sweater."

Griswold was a member of the United States Civil Rights Commission, but the idea of gender equity had not penetrated his comprehension. The first week of school, he invited the freshman women to his home and informed us that he was opposed to women attending law school but that the board had outvoted him. He said that the admissions committee counted the number of women in the class and then admitted that many additional men, certain that the women would never use their degrees and the world might otherwise be deprived of enough Harvard lawyers. Then he put us in folding chairs and ordered each of us to state why we were there, occupying . . . no, wasting such sacred space.

In stark terror, sitting uncomfortably on our chairs placed in a circle, each of us tried to sound profound and controlled in our answers. I said something trite and predictable like, "Oh, I am here to bolster my love of the law." But one of the women blithely said, "I'm here because I couldn't get into Yale." The dean grew so red in the face that I thought he might implode. He bellowed that such a thing was impossible, and the evening was *over*.

I had an absolutely miserable time at Harvard. The dorms had orange ceilings and brown walls, and the people had a lot of attitude. I always took my education seriously, but never myself. Many of the students were utterly humorless grinds, underlining their textbooks and making outlines of the underlining! The only bright part of law school was Jim, who came up to me one day in the frigid library and introduced himself. (Looking back on that time, Jim once remarked, "It was like *Love Story*, but you didn't die.") He had graduated from Princeton and then done three years in the navy. We hung out with a group of less exalted and patrician classmates, most of whom had gone to college on ROTC scholarships and served in the military. We married after the first year; our parents thought we were young and crazy. But in those days people still labored under the amusing misconception that two could live as cheaply as one.

We had a church wedding in Des Moines, Iowa, where I'd gone to high school, and a reception at the airport, where we left for a honeymoon in Estes Park, Colorado, near the Rocky Mountain National Park. When we

checked into our hotel, sitting in the lobby was our property law professor, W. Barton Leach, quite excited because
he now had a third and fourth for bridge. We hadn't
intended to spend our honeymoon playing cards with a
professor, but the dictum of law school was clear: If one of
the teachers said "Deal," you dealt.

I remember pushing a shopping cart through the
aisles of the Star Market in Boston during my last year at
Harvard when I learned that President Kennedy had been
shot. Before I heard the store manager's solemn voice
come over the public address system, there was so much
commotion among the shoppers that my first thought was:
I wonder if the store's being held up. The atmosphere in
Massachusetts, JFK's home state, was gruesome and
inconsolable. People were weeping in the streets and listening to dirge music on the radio for days. Our neighbors
had planned a party for Sunday that weekend and couldn't
decide whether to cancel or not. Finally they went ahead
with it, judging that people at least needed to get out
and see each other to break through the funereal
atmosphere.

It was a memory I was to return to over and over during my own career in politics. Along with so many of my
contemporaries, I had believed in the youth and vigor and
promise of the Kennedy presidency, and as I stumbled in
my efforts at improving government, I wondered what a
difference his uninterrupted term of office might have

made. It was also impossible not to think of Robert Kennedy when I was the object of a threatening note or call from an indignant and menacing unknown, a customary peril of political life. Like Bobby, I was a social reformer people either loved or hated.

Jim and I brought quite different experiences of family life to our marriage. His parents were older when he was born, and he spent his entire childhood in the same house in suburban Chicago. Although his mother had a master's degree in math, she deferred to her husband's career as a dentist and stayed home with her family, making perfect pie crusts and ironing perfectly starched shirts. She died of cancer in her forties, so I never met her. I'm sure a lawyer who didn't know the difference between Crisco and cold cream was not her idea of a daughter-in-law!

I wanted a family like the one I grew up in. My parents both had pastoral "Little House on the Prairie" childhoods in small Nebraska farm towns. Dad wanted to go to Harvard, but the local bank folded during the Depression. There was no savings and loan bailout in the 1930s, so he went to Kearney State Teachers College, where he met my mother. As newlyweds, they set off to find their fortunes in the west. Dad bought a logging concern. When the cook quit, my father said, "We're having a few friends over for dinner." Mother got stuck cooking for all the loggers. She used to make stacks of pancakes, put them in bushel baskets and slide them down the tables where they instantly disappeared.

Both of my parents were full of spunk, with a sense of adventure and willingness to take risks. Dad was a private pilot who bought wrecked planes and rebuilt them. Shortly after they were married, he brought home a Singer sewing machine and asked Mother to make fabric covers for the wings of a plane he was rebuilding—a challenging first sewing project.

I was born in Portland, Oregon, and probably would have spent my whole life there but for World War II. After Pearl Harbor, when the city was under blackout conditions, my father was running a small local airport. He was asked to fly along the coast and report anything he saw. We were government gypsies, moving all during the war. Dad was called up to teach flying in Kansas City at TWA's flight-training facilities. It was taken over by what was then the Army Air Corps. We were in Dallas when the war ended, and my father went to work in aviation insurance. We moved as better job offers came along to Hamilton, Ohio, and then to Des Moines, Iowa, where I went to high school. My mother found herself back at work, much to her surprise, teaching public school. Our house always looked like a bulletin board, with drawings of turkeys on Thanksgiving and grapefruits painted red like steroidal cherries on Washington's Birthday; every holiday was vigorously celebrated. Mother believed it was better to read a book than to dust it, and housekeeping was considered an equal-employment opportunity in our home. Mother had it right.

Des Moines in the fifties looked like a scene from *American Graffiti* or *Bye-Bye Birdie*. Teenage girls wore poodle skirts and ate at drive-in restaurants with waiters rollerskating out to the cars, and the most exciting thing to hit town was Elvis Presley. I tried hard to be hip, but I was always a little different. One Christmas, a cab drove up to the house delivering a present from my boyfriend: a live skunk. I named it Petunia. I loved it, as my boyfriend knew I would, but my parents were horrified. Since we were just about to leave for a holiday visit, we arranged for a neighbor to care for the skunk. She put it in her basement where it pulled out a brick and tunneled deep into the ground. When we came home my parents issued an ultimatum that the skunk had to go. We took it to an animal shelter with the unlikely name of the Dumb Friends League. They ran a picture of Petunia in the local paper under the rubric of "Pets Ready to Be Adopted," so my boyfriend found out that I had rejected his gift.

It was just assumed that my brother Mike and I would get pilot's licenses. Dad's position was: If we were going to fly *in* a plane, we should know *how* to fly one. (Sometimes I miss the most obvious things. My solo flight at age sixteen was hairy for that reason: My instructor weighed about three hundred pounds. His weight had helped bring the plane to the ground fairly fast. I had so much trouble with my first solo landing that the air traffic controllers were beginning to think they'd have to shoot me down! Finally I remembered to start my descent further out since the plane was lighter. The gravity of the situation missed me at first!)

Dad was a resourceful man who mowed the grass in his suit because he didn't want to waste time changing clothes. He hated to see his children idle. He was always dragging Mike and me out to hangars to help work on the wrecked planes he would rebuild and sell. He even suggested that my high school dates come over and work on one of his projects instead of going to the movies. On vacations he liked to fly up the Al-Can highway between Alaska and Canada, staying in Omni radio stations (fliers kept their radios tuned to a certain frequency to navigate). Each station had a little runway and rather primitive no-frills government-owned cabins where we could stay "as guests of the Queen." I don't think she knew we were there, or that they ever had a royal visit! If we got weathered in, we just found an empty hangar and waxed the plane. Sometimes we'd go to the airport, our destination unplanned, and ask, "Where's the weather good?" It was like being the child of Jonathan Livingston Seagull.

My father thought he could teach us the value of a dollar by insisting that we pay our own college tuition, so I worked my way through the University of Minnesota. My father's connections there enabled me to get a job doing what he did: flying to crash sites and assessing aviation losses. The university owned a fleet of small planes for its

ROTC program, which would have been available at no charge, but women were prohibited from flying in the ROTC. The university didn't like the federal government's restrictions, so I was allowed to rent them for ten dollars an hour. (A flying association nominated me for making the year's most dangerous landing, in winds that were so high the plane literally couldn't move forward.) Flying paid off because I made so much money my first year that I not only paid my tuition but bought a Lincoln. It was long and a bright pastel aqua. It looked like an Easter egg on wheels.

Originally I wanted to study aerodynamic engineering, but I had one of those guidance counselors who screamed, "No, no, you'll just be wasting your parents' money." I tried to explain it was *my* money. I caved and launched into a history major. It was assumed that I could always teach. I also took Chinese, a ferociously difficult course. We were taught to write the intricate Chinese characters by holding an egg in the writing hand. If you did it wrong, the shell broke and you had egg dripping from your arms and sleeves—the embarrassing Chinese equivalent of getting egg on your face. Chinese made me really listen because different tonal inflections can make one word take on many meanings. ("Ma" can mean mother, horse, linen or chicken pox, so you'd better be careful or you end up saying something unflatteringly equine about your mother.) But, it was a mental workout and made me confident I could tackle anything.

Everyone in Minnesota seemed to be blond and statuesque. I was practically the only brunette in the state, and it was one of the few places where people thought I was short. (At five-seven, I was almost a glandular case in a family where my mother is five feet tall and my grandmother was four-feet-eight.)

I graduated in three years. I was in a hurry to begin Life with a capital "L" as quickly as possible and didn't even bother to attend commencement—I paid an undergraduate thirty-five dollars to go through the line and get my diploma. Then I thought: *Hmmmm, the law. . . .* It seemed not too narrowing as a profession, with lots of options and possibilities.

I didn't have any hoity-toity notions about Harvard. Someone suggested I ought to go to a "national" law school unless I knew where I would end up living. Harvard seemed national. When I applied, I wasn't yet twenty-one years old and got in trouble signing my own bond for tuition. My mother was rather depressed that I went to Harvard—she was sure nobody would ever marry me and she'd never be a grandmother.

After Jim and I married, we wanted to finish law school before starting a family, but contraceptives were illegal in Massachusetts. We could get prescriptions for birth control pills at the student clinic but had to wait until we visited my folks in Iowa or Jim's dad in Illinois to have the prescriptions filled. If I'd ever been prosecuted and convicted for bringing birth control pills into Massachusetts, I would not be able to practice law in most states. Three years later, the Supreme Court ruled in the case of *Griswold v. Connecticut* that married couples throughout the country had the right to obtain contraceptives, overriding state laws preventing such access. When I tell young women that story today, they look at me like I rode to school on a pterodactyl.

When we graduated and moved to Denver, my pro bono legal work for Planned Parenthood was my effort to ensure that those bad old days never returned. One of the Planned Parenthood clinics was in a fairly remote part of the state with a largely rural and Hispanic clientele. The husbands of many clients came out of a macho culture and were challenged by seeing the name of the clinic on a phone pad. If their wives actually tried to avail themselves of the services, they often suffered violent repercussions. One of the wives was on the local board and came up with the idea of changing the name to the "Women's Clothing Exchange" so the men could "save face." We city folks were uncomfortable with such chicanery. We were able to get some male social workers to interview the men in the area, and they reported that a name change would be a simple way for the Hispanic culture to accept the clinic. And we decided it didn't constitute fraud because the husbands knew what the name masked but felt they could play along.

One weekend in Denver in the late 1980s, as I started out my usual Saturday-Sunday events, I heard on the radio that hundreds of people from Operation Rescue, which was having a huge convention in town, had encircled the Planned Parenthood clinic, shutting off access to clients. They were pushing people around and breaking windows. My reaction was: *Oh, no, you don't—I helped build this place.* "My schedule just got canceled," I said to the staffer working with me. We made a stop at the doughnut store before proceeding to the clinic, where I told the Denver police to get me inside. They did everything to discourage me, but finally acquiesced. "We're just going to sit here calmly and eat our doughnuts and write down what we see," I told the clinic staff hunkered down inside. Sitting together under "enemy fire," with people literally coming at us through the windows, I understood what the military means about the bonding of soldiers in a foxhole. The notes we took became useful when the "rescuers" threatened to sue the Denver police department, claiming that they had used excessive force. I volunteered to testify for the police, armed with my carefully delineated version of the facts. The lawsuit never materialized.

In 1966, I got pregnant. For the first three months, my only problem was morning sickness and getting cracker crumbs in bed. We bought a brand-new contemporary A-frame house at a great price from a builder who'd gone bankrupt. The living room had a soaring forty-foot ceiling, with the master bedroom perched on a balcony near the top. Several times after we moved in, I had come home from work and smelled gas. I'd called the repairman, who looked at the furnace and found nothing wrong. One night we had a dinner party, and all four of our friends were so tired they left by 9:30—highly unusual for this young and spirited crowd. We were so tired ourselves that we didn't protest and just dropped into bed. I got up several times during the night feeling nauseated, but attributed the feeling to predawn morning sickness. Later, I was awakened by a great racket. I looked over the balcony and saw Jim lying on the floor with his head bleeding. My own head felt very fuzzy, but I managed to get downstairs and open the door. A neighbor's beagle ran in and started licking Jim's head. The neighbor, who never slept, followed the dog and smelled the gas immediately. He got us outside and called an ambulance.

During the night, Jim had awakened and realized that something was wrong, but by then he was not thinking clearly. His solution had been to try to turn off the thermostat with a fireplace tool. Then he fell on the tool and cut his head. It turned out there was nothing wrong with the furnace itself, but the exhaust stack had not been installed properly. The A-frame roof didn't look right with a higher exhaust, so after county inspectors approved the construction, the builder lowered the stack for aesthetic reasons. When the wind blew from a certain direction, a vacuum was created and carbon monoxide backed into the house.

We were lucky to be alive—we could just as easily have slept through the night and been found dead. Our concern turned toward the possible effect of gas on the fetus. The doctors played straight with me and admitted they didn't know. This was before the age of CAT scans and amniocentesis, so for the rest of my pregnancy I obsessed. I had an uncle who'd been a military physician, and he helped us get army studies about gas, but there was no information. Six weeks before my due date, I went into labor.

Moments after Scott was delivered, the obstetrician asked for the name of our family neurosurgeon. We didn't *have* a neurosurgeon, but I was to get one soon: Scott's head was larger than normal, and there was concern that he might be hydrocephalic. I think his head must have been measured one thousand times over the next several months. It wasn't until Scott was six months old that he was finally given a clean bill of health, and Jim and I could breathe again. During that anxious time we had collected old baby books of all our relatives for comparisons of head sizes. It turned out that there are big heads on both sides of the family. Think of what my political opponents could do with that!

I was not apprehensive about having more children because the odds of another freak accident were a million to one. We'd moved to the city, away from the A-frame that had been the cause of our ordeal. (We also realized why young marrieds don't have forty-foot balconies: Envision the baby dangling by one toe.) Two years later I became pregnant again, and I was especially thrilled because my brother and his wife, Julie, were also expecting. But during the fourth month, I started to bleed. My obstetrician brushed it off, saying that I was "high-strung": That being a Harvard lawyer, I was having trouble adjusting to life as a housewife. I was so weak I couldn't argue. (Believe me, that's weak.)

Then my sister-in-law lost her baby. I began to worry more about my own pregnancy. A month later, eight weeks before my due date, I went into labor on a weekend when we had a house full of company to celebrate a cousin's homecoming from Vietnam. Jim drove me to the hospital, where I waited for twelve hours in a small room while the staff tried to locate my obstetrician. I kept buzzing the nurse to ask whether another doctor could look at me because I knew there was something terribly wrong. The nurse, who repeatedly claimed she went to high school with me, kept telling me to calm down, nothing was wrong, that there were plenty of women just like me having babies in the hospital and I would have to wait my turn. She wouldn't even let me near a phone, knowing that I'd try to track down some medical assistance myself and not wanting to risk the wrath of a doctor whose weekend plans would be interrupted.

Eventually my doctor did arrive. When I was taken to the delivery room in full labor, I heard him say, "Oh, my God, we should have done a cesarean." For the first time I learned I was carrying twins, a girl and a boy. The girl had died much earlier in the pregnancy. That was the cause of my hemorrhaging. The boy was born barely alive, weighing only four and a half pounds. We tried to get him into Children's Hospital, which was better equipped to deal with preemies (Denver has a lot of premature births because of the altitude), but all the incubators were full. When the doctors told us that his brain had hemorrhaged due to the difficult delivery, we stipulated, sobbing over our decision, that no heroic measures should be taken. The baby died the next morning from complications of a difficult delivery. I was put in a ward with another woman who had given birth to a healthy child. She was bursting with joy but tried to cork it because of me. The nurses wouldn't move me. I couldn't stand it, so I just put on my clothes, called a cab, and went home. I figured they knew where to send the bills.

This second pregnancy had been an intense, draining and humiliating nightmare. I was angry at the doctor for refusing to listen to me, but I was angry at myself for putting up with it. Here I was, a trained lawyer, letting a doctor convince me I had no right to question his judgment about *my* pregnancy and *my* baby. He intimidated me and made me feel petty and powerless. The hospital staff put me in a position of surrendering all control. I vowed never again and decided to act on my anger. I began shopping around for a new doctor, asking questions until I met one who treated me like a thinking human being rather than a receptacle or a mental case.

Changing doctors made a world of difference. My next pregnancy, in 1970, was a pleasant, uneventful nine months. But two days after I brought my newborn daughter home, I was back in the hospital with uncontrollable bleeding. My doctor was preparing to do a hysterectomy but decided I was too weak and resorted to the rather primitive method of stuffing me with hundreds of yards of gauze. I was in the hospital for the next five weeks, spending my thirtieth birthday in intensive care. Floating in and out of consciousness, I was certain I was going to die. It was a Catholic hospital and they even gave me last rites. I never got a proper diagnosis; I'd already lost so much blood that nothing extra was done. It would have been foolhardy. When I was finally recovered and strong enough to undergo tests, they couldn't catch me. As I left the hospital, my doctor warned, "I don't ever want to see you pregnant again. Another baby could kill you."

There was other fallout from my childbirth experience. All those blood transfusions left me with what is now called hepatitis C. When my condition was first discovered in the House physician's office, there was no name for it. Up until the 1980s it was called "non-A, non-

B hepatitis." Luckily, it has not given me any problems, and I've been healthier and more energetic than most. But any time I have to see a new doctor, he or she goes into orbit. There is no cure at this point. I can't get life insurance because if I ever do have real problems, it's death or a liver transplant.

Doctors left no doubt in my mind that I should not have another child. I knew many other women had equally compelling reasons to avoid a pregnancy. Contrary to conventional wisdom, pregnancy is not a nine-month cruise. My experiences reinforced my belief that a woman has a right to decide what happens to her own body. That right should not be curtailed by the government. In the conservatives' agenda, the minute a woman becomes pregnant, she should turn off her brain. They want to deny her any right to decide what is best for herself or any children she might conceive. In fact, once conception occurs, the woman is rarely mentioned again—she's just an impersonal receptor. The fetus is assigned a full-blown personality: Girls are holding dolls in the womb and boys are playing with trucks.

On January 22, 1973, during my first month in Congress, the Supreme Court handed down its landmark decision on a woman's right to choose whether or not to have a baby. Overnight, *Roe v. Wade* made a woman's right to an abortion the law of the land and virtually eliminated illegal "back room" butchers, with their alarmingly high mortality rates. Even though seventeen states already had laws making some abortions legal and nearly 600,000 women had obtained legal abortions in 1972, the Centers for Disease Control estimated that another 130,000 women had had to resort to illegal or self-induced procedures that year. *Roe v. Wade* sparked a fervent nationwide debate that rages to this day. I have been in the middle of that debate my entire legislative career. This was never an enjoyable task, but my own story made me tenacious about it.

The choice debate was one nobody on my side wanted to enter and one the other side couldn't wait to jump on. Whenever the issue came to the House floor, which seemed to be weekly, many of the men would ask the women why we kept making them vote on this politically poisonous matter. Even though our male supporters knew better, they held the congresswomen responsible for the frequency of the debate. I personalized the antichoice attacks. I felt they were saying that women have such dark hearts and shallow minds, we would always be tempted to have an abortion just to fit into a party dress unless the government prohibited us from doing it. Many seemed to feel that if Congress didn't mandate motherhood, women were so frivolous they'd jettison pregnancies at will. Often I escaped to the congresswomen's lounge with dry heaves after those bruising debates, but the worst time was when I painfully recounted my own childbirth experiences, hoping to enlighten certain colleagues who seemed to think pregnancy was simple. I was stunned when some responded that if I was "malformed," I should have had a hysterectomy. But this debate was a a high-stakes political debate—no one wanted facts.

In the wake of *Roe v. Wade*, abortions became a mortal battlefield on which conservatives and progressives fought out the definition of women's roles in society. Both sides understood that the Supreme Court decision was as much about an individual woman's right to determine what happened to her body as it was about an unwanted pregnancy. With the legal authority to make decisions about childbearing, women gained power over their own lives. That scared a lot of people. The debate became volatile because right-to-life organizations were extremely graphic in their depiction of abortion. They deluged congressional offices with postcards of aborted fetuses, not bothering to disclose that most of the pictures derived from advanced pregnancies, much further along than the vast majority of women who choose abortion would be. They made misleading films and created simple slogans out of hard questions, cavalierly labeling as a killer anyone who advocated women being allowed to choose. It seemed the conservatives had a fast breeder antiabortion amendment reactor that kept producing amendments prohibiting abortions on interstate highways, in federal prisons or whatever else they could cook up.

Despite the preempting of the term by the conservatives, I was and am, like many women, both pro-life and pro-choice. Obviously I wanted a family—I had to struggle to have babies, and my children are the source of my strength. But I feel that every woman has to make her own decision about family size, depending on her circumstances, religious beliefs and medical advice. The notion that a woman would choose abortion casually is anathema to me. If there really is a small percentage of women using abortion as a form of birth control, then we need to educate them about safe and reliable options, not deny choice to the rest of the population.

The Congressional Caucus on Women's Issues that I cochaired did not become pro-choice until 1992. It broke my heart, but we had to appease colleagues such as Lindy Boggs of Louisiana, and Mary Rose Oakar and Marcy Kaptur, both of Ohio—all Democrats who would have quit the caucus over religious convictions if we went pro-choice. Since there were so few women in Congress, I felt it was better to hang together on other issues where we had consensus rather than break apart. A separate bipartisan group was put together to whip the choice issue.

I worked with the National Abortion Rights Action League to collect personal stories from women who chose abortion in tragic circumstances. I then asked colleagues to read letters from such women during a congressional session. One letter was from a woman whose aunt had died from a back-alley abortion, another from a teenager who said she felt she had only two choices: abortion or suicide. These experiences illustrated how difficult an abortion is and reminded us there are more lives involved than the potential life of a fetus. I don't think it is within my power or that of any other lawmaker to decide which life has the greater claim: that of an embryo or its mother. "Choose life" sounds great as a bumper sticker, but *whose* life do we choose?

Unfortunately, neither these stories nor opinion polls showing strong public support for a woman's right to abortion have overcome the strength of the right-to-life movement when it comes to influencing Congress. These groups have been able to prohibit government funding of abortions and add antiabortion restrictions to legislation. Over the years, they have curtailed the abortion rights of forty million Americans, including low-income women, federal employees, military personnel, retirees and their dependents, Native American women, Peace Corps volunteers and teenage girls. I wish that, instead of their anti-woman efforts, they would join in supporting research to discover a safe, totally reliable and user-friendly contraceptive so the question of abortion would be moot. Most also don't support any aid for the baby after it's born. Barney Frank used to say that they believed life began at conception and ended at birth. I'm amazed how willing the right is to stick their heads in the sand about teenage pregnancy. The fact is that sexual activity among teens is increasing, and the United States has the highest teenage pregnancy rate of any developed country. Recently some conservatives came up with the brilliant solution of asking for federal money to set up chastity clinics. What does the federal government know about chastity? You have to know something to teach it. I'd rather see money used for community forums where foreign students and American students who have lived abroad could share their knowledge of how other countries deal with teenage sexuality. We clearly don't have the answer.

Every year a great many babies are born to teens, most of them unmarried girls under the age of eighteen. The personal and social costs to these new parents are staggering. We have only begun to feel the cost to society. On economic grounds alone, it is hard to see how we will be able to care for and educate these children in generations to come. So many of the most rabid right-to-lifers don't address this question. In the global economy of the twenty-first century, we will need more education, not less.

Curbing teenage pregnancy is not simple. Education is clearly one factor. We have practically no comprehensive sex education in our schools in this country. We must have it. Parents say they want to do it, but most don't. We should combine information on contraception with lessons on sexual responsibility. The National Research Council issued a report for 1987 that pointed out the connection between teens' sexual activity, including their use of birth control, and their perceptions of their lives and prospects. The brighter they saw their future, the more likely they were to be sexually responsible.

Our challenge is to make being pregnant "uncool." Teenagers are bombarded with messages of sexuality from television, music, movies and magazines. They seldom see the consequences of youthful sexuality, the strain of pregnancy and new parenthood on young lives, or the lingering and sometimes fatal effects of sexually transmitted disease. When I visit programs for teen mothers in schools and young women's residences, the girls consistently tell me that they didn't realize what motherhood would be like. A Boston doctor told me that she had seen many young girls give up their babies after a couple of weeks because they were so overwhelmed by the responsibility of caring for them. There are some innovative programs trying to convey the constant accountability babies require to teens before they get pregnant: Girls (and boys) carry around a ten-pound sack of flour and are tethered to its perpetual "care." We've got to keep creating such imaginative programs, and broadcast reality into teen culture.

In order for teens to practice responsible sexual behavior, they need information. Our current system presents obstacles to kids trying to learn about birth control. A Supreme Court ruling gave school authorities the right to censor student newspaper articles written on teen pregnancy. Amendments to Title X, passed during the Reagan

On an Israeli military base. Oops! My rear was bigger than I thought and I didn't make it through the fence.

Armed Services colleagues at the Golan Heights in Israel.

A windy day in Bethlehem—but wind beats bullets anytime!

In Jerusalem with colleagues
from the Armed Services
Committee.

Egyptian President Anwar Sadat, an
amazing man whose early death
was a huge global loss.

A group of Armed Services colleagues waiting to see a Saudi prince. Note: I had to wear my raincoat because I had packed short sleeves (it was hot), and short sleeves were verboten. In fact, I wore my raincoat for all three days we were there.

King Faisal of Saudi Arabia. I was the first woman he ever shook hands with. He was shot and killed a few months after this photograph was taken.

Peggy Heckler (holding a child), me, Olympia Snowe, and Lindy Boggs at a Cambodian refugee camp in 1979. This was truly a life-changing experience for all of us. So many children looking for their families forced us to realize the chaos war brings to everyone.

A visit to an Afghan camp. Notice: No women are sitting on the ground. They took me to a tent and held me there so the only part of the official meetings I saw was the photos. They didn't even send their girls to school. They are now running Afghanistan and the leaders of Iran have called them extremists.

In Vietnam, trying to get more information about U.S. MIAs and POWs from Vietnamese officials. This guy looks like he's scared to death of me.

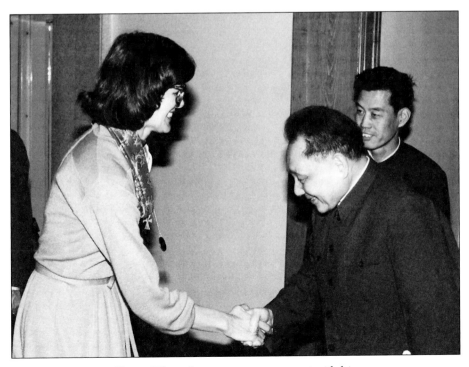

Deng Xiao Ping in China. When the congresswomen met with him, every time Bella Abzug said something, he let a wad of tobacco fly into a spittoon.

Escorting a Colorado Princess in my rabbit suit. Who would guess this suit could cause me such political grief?

At the American Embassy in Beijing. I was a hit there but was savaged at home for being so juvenile.

Listening to congressional testimony.

Randall Robinson and me at a press conference on South Africa and Nelson Mandela. There were many of these.

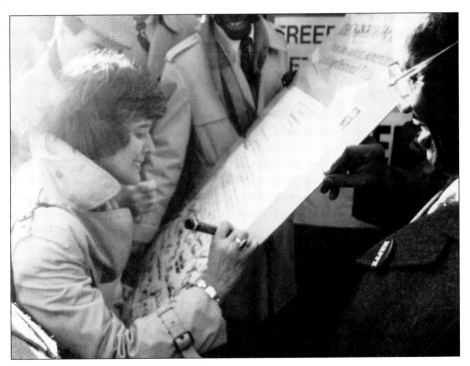

During the Reagan era, we pushed hard on South African issues because the Reagan administration was protecting apartheid. Here I am signing a Free South Africa letter in front of the South African embassy.

King Hussein of Morocco (left) with a U.S. delegation. Clearly you do not want to wear a print dress here!

With Sandra Day O'Connor.

With Barbara Bush, Nancy Reagan and Margaret Heckler at a luncheon given by the Congressional Caucus on Women's Issues. Ladies who lunch are not in Congress! This was our last lunch with Mrs. Reagan because substance was not allowed on the menu.

With Geraldine Ferraro and Jean Stapleton of *All in the Family*. Jean was a great supporter of the congresswomen and the first to say "breast cancer" on a national TV show.

Former California governor Jerry Brown was a magnet for college students. He fed off their energy and questions.

Meeting with Cesar Chavez of the United Farm Workers. He was so committed to the people he represented. It was a great antidote to cynicism.

At the 1984 Democratic convention. One could get a nosebleed!

I was cochair of Gary Hart's 1984 and 1988 presidential campaigns, and lived through both—barely.

Family photo in Colorado.

Portraying Edith Wilson in a play, 1978. Princeton calls its computer system "Edith" after Mrs. Wilson because it runs the university and she ran the government when Woodrow was incapacitated!

Congressman Charles Wilson
of Texas, a Democrat
elected with me in 1972.
He campaigned with
personalized gun rags and
called me "Babycakes"
all twenty-four years.
"Unreconstructed"
is a word I'd
attach to him!

In New York with Jim and
Nora Dunn, who did a terrific
impression of me on *Saturday
Night Live*. Suddenly Jim had
two wives!

A navy trainer in Pensacola, Florida, one Mother's Day.

Ready to fly! At 30,000 feet we see why God is so patient with us. The world looks much calmer from the air.

Navy trainer. The guys in Tailhook do not like this picture!

Posing for a picture with some of the enlisted men from Colorado in the Demilitarized Zone, South Korea. The military was great at getting together soldiers who wanted their photos taken. Then you could send them to their folks.

Visiting the Denver Naval Reserve Base. Somehow, I think admirals would enter differently.

administration, contained the "squeal rule," a regulation stipulating that parents must be notified before a teenager is given contraceptives at any clinic that gets federal funds. We often treat our children as if they are hothouse plants. We want to filter everything and protect them. Some believe that giving young people information about sex encourages them to have sex. I think it encourages them to act responsibly.

Statistics show that teenage parents are more likely than other teens to come from poor families and more apt to drop out of school, passing on the sad legacy of poverty to the next generation. The Children's Defense Fund found that young women who were poor and had below-average academic skills were five and a half times more likely than other teenage girls to get pregnant. For these young women, we need to redouble our efforts to keep abortions safe and legal, ensuring that those who depend on federal assistance have the same reproductive health rights and access to information and services as middle-class girls and women. But we must emphasize that informed, sensible and responsible behavior, not abortion, is the best form of birth control. We must instill hope in a brighter future. That's the best motivator not to become pregnant.

Legislators didn't stop at dictating to teens. They passed a gag rule that kept medical professionals from discussing abortions with women of *any* age. I fear some believed that if women even heard about abortion, they would want one. Our foreign policy on this subject is a ridiculous legacy of the Reagan years. Shortly after Reagan came to office, an international family planning meeting hosted by the United Nations was held in Mexico City, and the United States announced it would support only "natural" family planning. Overseas, any voluntary organization that got federal foreign aid money, such as Planned Parenthood or the Agency for International Development, was restricted to teaching the rhythm method. This became known as the "Mexico City policy." In Colorado we called people who used the rhythm system "parents."

It seems to me that if Congress is going to scream about out-of-control immigration, it should at least listen to countries asking us to help them limit the number of future immigrants. Spending tax money for worthless programs is nuts. Natural family planning is a joke, so don't waste my tax dollars on it. This crazy policy was finally reversed by Congress in February 1997 by a razor-thin majority. It must stay reversed; environmentalists should be a lot more active in the family planning debates. They can plant all the trees they want, but if the world population doubles in twenty years, it won't matter.

After Congress barely reversed the Mexico City policy in 1997, it then refused to fund the International Monetary Fund (IMF) in the middle of the Asian economic crisis unless President Clinton reinstated the policy. He refused. Congress adjourned for Thanksgiving and Christmas without paying our IMF share. So much for world leadership.

Public policy should provide options for people who want to limit their family size, and it should also extend choices to those who want a family but are unable to have one. Infertility and the new reproductive technologies will be important family health issues of the twenty-first century. Infertility strikes at least one in five American couples, yet it is ignored as a legitimate health issue. Insurance companies often deem it extraneous to health care. The press often portrays it as a "yuppie" problem. There are plenty of people who still believe all you have to do to have babies is relax. The number of couples unable to conceive is increasing. The infertility rate among married women twenty to twenty-four years old has tripled in the past twenty years. Infertility is not just a women's problem: It still takes two.

Just as the cost of pregnancy and delivery should not discourage people from pursuing their commitment to parenthood, the expense of treating infertility should not place children beyond the reach of prospective parents. Health insurance makes it possible for most couples to afford a family, but not the infertile couple. Their effort to have a child is at great personal expense, with no guarantee of success, and these desperate would-be parents often grasp expensive, unproven methods of treatment. People are mortgaging their houses and rolling in mud—anything to have a baby.

The price of fertility treatment may be high when shouldered by individuals, but it would add little (approximately one-tenth of 1 percent) to the nation's health-care bill if covered by insurance. As chair of the Civil Service Subcommittee, I proposed legislation requiring the companies that insure federal workers to cover the costs of infertility treatment. Insurers object because they claim that fertility treatment is not health-related; but they cover vasectomy and tubal ligation. They also say that fertility treatment is overly costly, but cost is not a justification for discrimination. In states that have already passed laws mandating coverage by insurance companies (Massachusetts, Texas, Hawaii, Arkansas and Maryland), costs for fertility treatment are far lower than what was projected.

Infertility is a controversial subject right now. It is largely an unregulated and lucrative business, and women are not being fully informed about risks. But we'd have better controls if we medicalize it. Having reproductive organs that aren't working properly is no different than having any other kind of organ that isn't functioning.

Another option for childless couples is adoption, but it too is a long, costly and uncertain process. Many adoption agencies have requirements concerning a couple's age, religion and financial status. If accepted, the couple must go through a waiting period that may last five years or more. Often there is little advance notice when a baby finally becomes available. Once a child is found, the couple must immediately come up with a large sum of money. Adoption costs, which run into tens of thousands of dollars, are usually not covered by insurance.

My legislation to have insurance companies cover infertility treatments would also cover the costs of adoption. To come up with this proposal, I worked with an unlikely ally, Senator Gordon Humphrey (Republican from New Hampshire), one of the most outspoken advocates in Congress for the right-to-life organizations. In 1987 we were able to pass into law a two-year test program to reimburse members of the military. Their efforts to adopt are further complicated by the military's frequent tour-of-duty moves and low pay. After two years it was canceled because a congresswoman took over the Military Personnel Committee. She had been adopted herself, and I think she emotionally interpreted this law as sending a message that prospective parents need an incentive to adopt. I disagree. So we allow tax relief for breeding thoroughbred horses, but not for adopting children? That makes no sense.

It wasn't until the new crop of congresswomen arrived in 1992 that we were able to get some momentum on pro-choice issues in the Women's Caucus. Suddenly 10 percent of Congress was female. On swearing-in day in January 1993, as I was beaming at all my new colleagues in skirts, one of the old bulls said to me, "Look what you've done. The place looks like a shopping center." Where did he shop where 90 percent of the shoppers were male?

This fresh new group had attitude and wanted action. We got it. We passed our backlogged bills and Reagan/ Bush vetoes, and Clinton signed them. It was a heady time. Then came the angry white male backlash election of 1994. A lot of the new women in Congress lost. Polls later showed that many women who had voted in 1992 didn't bother to vote in 1994, no longer feeling threatened. Never forget that politics and democracy need constant maintenance.

The Republican majority of 1994 was terrified that women now had access to information about family planning and abortion on the Internet, in the privacy of their own homes. And if RU-486 could allow women to have abortions in their homes, the right wing would lose its focal point. Where would they picket? United in fear, they figured out a way to put Internet conversations under the Comstock Act. Anthony Comstock was a special unpaid agent of the Post Office in the late 1800s who worried that the U.S. postal service could allow birth control and abortion information to flow freely into private homes. He persuaded Congress to pass legislation criminalizing such mailings, got the act named after himself and then got Congress to give him the authority to enforce it. He approached his task with a vengeance, getting Margaret

Sanger, the courageous founder of Planned Parenthood, jailed along with her husband.

In the middle of this century, Congress removed the birth control provisions from the Comstock Act, but the criminal sanctions for passing information about abortion remain. When the huge telecommunications bill was passed in 1994, the Comstock Act was attached by reference through a legal sleight of hand: As a bill is about to pass, a group of congressmen with special interests can say, "We hereby attach U.S. Statute Number So-and-so." Unless you happen to carry the Federal Code around with you in your dump truck, you have no immediate way of knowing what's being tacked on. Very sneaky. That's what Henry Hyde (Republican from Illinois) and his buddies did with the Comstock Act. When it was discovered, many members were furious. When confronted, Hyde said it was a mistake. We then organized to have it removed on Corrections Day, the time set aside to set right earlier wrongs, but Hyde would never give the go-ahead signal. My conclusion is he and his colleagues knew full well what they were doing. The mere threat that discussing abortion over the Internet could be criminal activity is a real inhibitor, a cyber gag rule. Treating women as adults is a radical concept for a majority in Congress!

Next the conservatives rallied around something they called "late-term abortion," using charts paid for by religious advocacy groups. The impression was created that women well along in a pregnancy would wake up one day and have a whimsical "change of heart." In fact women who had these procedures were usually joyously antici-pating a new addition to their family and their dream exploded. They chose abortion only because something had gone dreadfully wrong with the pregnancy. These women were savaged and dismissed by Congress because they did not fit the fictional portrait of women conserva-tives wanted to portray. President Clinton listened to them and bravely vetoed the bill.

My last year in Congress, I introduced the Safe Moth-erhood Act, a concept that has not been the focus of national attention for decades. The United States doesn't even have accurate statistics on maternal deaths because the numbers are collected by individual states. Each state has different criteria. In other countries, if a woman dies within a year of having a baby, they look carefully to see if it was related to childbirth, but in the United States "maternal death" usually means only a death during labor or on the delivery table. If a new mother dies of some complication, they tend to record the complication as the cause, not childbirth.

We do know that the healthiest pregnancies are intended pregnancies. The Safe Motherhood Act would provide for a standardization of statistics and for more research about maternal health. Our mortality rates are disgraceful. Even in the military, where pregnant women are probably the most fit human specimens in the country, there is a high incidence of admission to the hospital with predelivery problems. I was thrilled when I heard that Congressman John Dingell (Democrat from Michigan) is the lead sponsor of this bill in the new Congress. It is my hope that he may be able to build a bipartisan bridge to pass the bill. It should be of concern to everyone in Congress. I understand that, even though politicians think they are self-made, they all had mothers.

5

Family Values

The business of politics as usual, however protracted
and recalcitrant, was easy compared to the challenge
of juggling career and family. Sleep deprivation was the
theme of my early years in Congress. There were no support groups for working moms in 1972. My father had
advised a swanlike illusion: paddling like mad under the
water, while projecting the image of gliding above it. (Every
now and then I still get a message from a friend saying my
frantically paddling feet are above the waterline, and I
know to slow down.) Politicians love to talk about family
values, but their grandiloquence is a perfect reflection of
our societal dilemma: We want Norman Rockwell images
of hearth and home, but personal immersion in family life
is tough. Ronald Reagan was our nation's first divorced
president. Suddenly the new measure for family values was
the depth of one's rhetoric, not practicing commitment.

There's always been a double standard for married women in politics. Early on, I got in great political trouble when I was asked, "How can you be both a congresswoman and a mother?" and I replied, "I have a brain and a uterus, and they both work." This double standard took out Congresswoman Coya Knutson, the first and last woman ever elected to Congress from Minnesota. Knutson, the daughter of Norwegian immigrants, was inspired to get into politics by the example of Eleanor Roosevelt. She sang her own campaign song in 1953, accompanying herself on the accordion. There was just a handful of women in Congress when she arrived on the scene like a human tornado, the classic overachiever. She fiercely championed family farms, got the first federal funding for cystic fibrosis research, produced the first bill calling for income tax checkoffs to finance presidential elections, and originated the bill that led to the federally financed student loan program. When did she sleep?

She also found time to dye her hair and buy some stylish clothes, which did not sit well with some of her constituents in a conservative Lutheran district. They decided that she was wild with Capitol fever. After two terms, the Democratic-Farmer-Labor Party refused to endorse her again. She was forced to run in a primary, which she won. Then some political enemies got her husband to sign an infamous "Coya Come Home Letter," which was published in newspapers and pasted on billboards across her state. The letter asked her to leave Congress and return to what he described as "the happy home we once enjoyed." Mr. Knutson was a farmer who had dropped out of school in the seventh grade and became an abusive alcoholic— Coya used to wear dark glasses to hide her black eyes. Her husband later tried to retract the letter, saying her critics got him drunk before he signed it, but it was too late. People viewed Coya as a callous, uncaring wife who abandoned her husband for naked ambition. She lost the election to a Republican opponent who used the slogan "A Big Man for a Man-Sized Job." Four years later she divorced her husband, but she never spoke publicly against him.

Tip O'Neill and other congressmen recognized that Coya had a lot of talent and went to Minnesota to offer help. The local Democratic Party had dumped her like damaged goods. Minnesota has never elected another woman to Congress; only Mrs. Hubert Humphrey was appointed for the interim period between her husband's death and the next election, but she retired rather than run. When Coya Knutson died in 1996, her son, one of her biggest supporters, said he was amazed that his mother never expressed bitterness against his father or the party.

I always think of Coya Knutson as a cautionary tale. The standards for women in politics are still higher than they are for men. Absolute measurements are impossible because in every part of the country the bar is in a different place. I suspect that a woman in public office any-where in the United States would be dead meat if the equivalent of a Gennifer Flowers or Paula Jones or a twenty-one-year-old male intern challenged her private life.

Political wives since the days of Caesar have always had to seem squeaky clean, but husbands are new to the game.

When I was elected to Congress, Jim decided to err on the side of caution, not wanting to supply my political enemies with even a hint of impropriety or bad judgment on his part. When I was considering a run for the presidency, he asked the *Legal Times* law journal to examine all the dealings at his law firm for any possible conflict of interest. It gave him rave reviews, but from day one he told his partners he would not do anything that looked like lobbying. He often turned down the prospects of megabucks because there were plenty of special-interest groups that would have paid dearly for access to a man whose pillow talk with a congresswoman could aid their cause. When we got married, Jim had indulged his love of foreign cars, but once I was in office he said, "We're going to drive American." And we pay more taxes than anyone we know, just sucking it up and following the tax code to the letter. Marriage has cost Jim a lot. He loves to point out my "little hobby" spills over into his life and net worth every day.

Everyone brings expectations to a marriage—I'm sure Jim never expected he'd be sleeping with a congresswoman.

But he has always been my biggest booster and never made his support contingent on his needs being met. Our standard joke was, "When are we going to get a wife?" but he never said, "Your career is on hold till we get one of my shirts ironed." Plenty of professional women were making jams and jellies at 3:00 A.M. because they thought they owed it to their spouse for the privilege of working outside the home. Jim was lucky if he got store-bought jelly on a peanut butter sandwich; microwave popcorn was a homecooked meal. In the day-to-day maintenance of a marriage, I favored the Julia Child approach over the unattainable and glossy perfection of Martha Stewart. Julia Child is a *human* role model: She drops the roast chicken on the floor and says, "Not to worry, I have another one just like it in the kitchen." Our house was never a page out of *House Beautiful,* but after my election I had a great excuse for the way it looked. I was doing House work elsewhere. The press would ask what my biggest fear was, and I always answered, "Losing our housekeeper." It was a real fear because without one, the Environmental Protection Agency could declare our home a Superfund site.

In the mid-eighties, the *Washington Post* did an article on Department of Health and Human Services Deputy Secretary Constance Horner, and her husband suggested starting a Denis Thatcher Society for men married to powerful women. Margaret Thatcher's husband never responded, but mine did. The Thatcherites were launched, with their official motto being "Yes, dear." Jim and Charles Horner, a right-wing Republican, made an odd couple, but they gathered others and would meet for an occasional lunch. The rule was they only met where they could sign their wives' names on the bill. When Denis Thatcher himself came to town, the two were invited by the British Embassy to meet him in a receiving line. They introduced themselves with a few words of explanation about the Society. Thatcher's response, with a typically British stiff upper lip, was "Indeed?" But the embassy kept them plugged in, and from time to time Jim would get calls saying that the Thatchers were planning to visit Washington, and would the "Society" like to meet with Mr. Thatcher? *People* magazine even photographed him sitting outside the British Embassy with cutouts of the Thatchers.

Part of the key to our successful marriage was that going to law school together taught us how to fight without personalizing or internalizing. When we graduated, the year after another Harvard alumnus, John F. Kennedy, was assassinated, a classmate wrote in my yearbook: "For a brief time our generation has had its hand upon the rudder of national destiny. For a moment it appeared as though our venerable institutions and conventional mythology were to be reexamined and revitalized. Perhaps we, like the generation that followed Lincoln, shall turn away from paths illumined by the late president, turn inward in pursuit of private security or backward in conformity to comfortable, if hardly serviceable, ideas."

The week that I went to the Middle East during my first year in Congress was the tenth anniversary of Kennedy's death. I kept thinking about his love of Robert Frost and the poet's memorable lines about two paths diverging in the woods: "I took the one less traveled by / And that has made all the difference." When I returned from the trip, my husband had left this note on my pillow: "Keep on your path, Patricia, the one less traveled, the one illumined by courage and marked by critical examination of our institutions and mythology." Clearly, being treasured at home freed me to be strong and brave in public. I wish there could be an entitlement program ensuring every American a supportive life partner. I could draft the bill, maybe even get it passed, but I don't know how to enforce it.

Jim and I had a common vision for our family: We wanted the children woven into our daily lives. The words are easy, but the weaving is hard. Neither of us wanted to be the disciplinarian or the heavy. Both of us volunteered to be the good cop, so how to proceed? We came up with the concept of "Team Family." We negotiated with Scott and Jamie just as management does with players. Our goal was for them to discipline themselves. We had actual signed documents like the Hound Agreement (to get a dog), different Sibling Peace Treaties, and other innovative contracts. Our child-rearing techniques were slightly legalistic, but what can you expect from two lawyers?

Naturally, the children figured out ways to bend or circumvent the rules, but so do adults. It's amazing how they learn at such a young age to play us and our guilt. When they were still very little, I overheard Scott counseling Jamie, "Never tell Mom and Dad you 'want' something. Say 'need.'"

There was one absolute canon: The kids had to do well in school. We explained we would love to have them travel with us. But we didn't have enough money for both travel and private school tuition. There are no funds for congressional family travel. Consequently members' families are usually parked back home in the district or left in Washington. Our kids had a choice: If they got good grades in public school, the family coffers could be spent on travel. If their report cards suffered, the money would go for private school.

The plan worked. The kids loved having their travel accounts. They became real self-starters about studying, and their exposure to the world was immense.

My campaign slogan was "She wins, we win," and our family slogan was, "She goes, we go," the four of us bouncing gleefully through time zones—Europe, Asia and all over the United States. We went to Germany before the Berlin Wall came down, and the guards did what we hoped they would do: give us a civics lesson. They detained us for hours, despite the fact that I was traveling under my personal, not my congressional, passport. One Thanksgiving when the kids were twelve and eight, we worked in the refugee camps of Thailand, where Jim had gone on business. The Red Cross was handing out cooking kits, and thousands of refugees had walked hundreds of miles to receive them. There weren't nearly enough for all who had come. The classic bureaucratic response was: It was nice of these people to walk here, but because we don't have enough kits, we have to send the refugees back. We decided to rip open the bags and divvy the stuff up. Everyone got something. Riding to the Cambodian border in a blue-and-white U.N. jeep, we saw three Vietnamese tanks through the trees. "This is reality," I said to my children, "and this is what pushed these people into the camps." One young man approached us and asked if we would be his sponsors to enter the United States. He already had a skill, glass cutting. We did sponsor him and his siblings while he got settled in Denver.

As a family, we will never forget those experiences. The kids said what surprised them the most was the vast expanse of refugees as far as the eye could see. At home, these people just flickered across a TV screen. Scott and Jamie met refugees who were members of the royal family, lawyers, journalists, and teachers. Scott said, "None of them ever thought they would be a refugee." He was right.

At the time I worried about whether I should expose my kids to this. In retrospect, it was the best thing we ever did as a family. We went totally outside our middle-class bubble and learned how precious life is, and how tenuous our grasp of it is.

The kids also visited classified nuclear weapon sites on military bases and distributed fliers at political conventions. Sometimes they felt like science fair projects when reporters wanted to interview them and find out how warped they were by having such a weird mother and family. They straightened the reporters out in short order.

When I say the whole family went away together, I mean the *whole* family. Often we traveled with dogs and even a pet bunny, Franklin Delano Rabbit. Before each trip I used to drive to the vet for FDR's health certificate thinking: *How much is it costing to have this animal's temperature taken?* On one flight back to Denver, there was already a pet in the tourist cabin where we were sitting, so Franklin was tucked under a seat up in first class. A kindly lady decided that the cute bunny could be trusted to get out and nibble some of her salad. Franklin broke for freedom, and the kids had to run from the rear of the plane to catch him. Dignity and power are deep-sixed as you crawl on airplane floors while pursuing family pets!

I wanted Scott and Jamie to feel that Denver was home and yet keep them with me during the week in Washington. There were great advantages to having them schooled in Washington because they didn't have to deal with "My dad thinks your mom is a jerk" stuff. Certainly plenty of people in Washington thought I was a jerk, but it was a big city and kids didn't know about politicians from Colorado.

I often found myself going to guilty extremes to be a more traditional mom. When Scott was in first grade, his school had a bake sale. I came home from work very late and set about making a cake (out of a box, of course). The next day, I asked him how the bake sale went. "Fine," he said, "but the rich kids just brought money." I realized he didn't care if his mother was Betty Crocker.

In the 1950s when I was in high school, home economics was a required course. It was my lowest grade. Early on I learned homemaking was *not* my calling: We had to darn socks. With each stitch, the hole in my sock got bigger instead of smaller, so I darned a non-hole. It looked beautiful, but the teacher discovered my subterfuge, and I failed sock-darning.

One of our textbooks listed rules for marriage that I reconstructed with some friends not long ago. Read this and you'll know why home economics gave me great trouble.

How to Be a Good Wife

Have dinner ready. Plan ahead, even the night before, to have a delicious meal — on time. This is a way of letting him know you have been thinking of him and care about his needs. Most men are hungry when they come home, and the prospect of a good meal is part of the welcome needed.

Prepare yourself. Take fifteen minutes to rest so that you are refreshed when he arrives. Touch up your makeup, put a ribbon in your hair and be fresh-looking. He has just been with a lot of work-weary people. Be a little gay and a little more interesting. His boring day may need a lift.

Clear away the clutter. Make one last trip through the main part of the house just before your husband arrives, gathering up schoolbooks, toys, paper, etc. Then run a dust cloth over the tables. Your husband will feel he has reached a haven of rest and order, and it will give you a lift too.

Prepare the children. Take a few minutes to wash the children's hands and faces if they are small, comb their hair and, if necessary, change their clothes. They are little treasures, and he would like to see them playing the part.

Minimize all noise. At the time of his arrival, eliminate all noise of the washer, dryer, dishwasher or vacuum. Try to encourage the children to be quiet. Be happy to see him, and greet him with a smile.

Some don'ts: Don't greet him with problems or complaints. Don't complain if he's late for dinner. Count this as minor compared with what he might have done that day. Make him comfortable. Have him lean back in a comfortable chair or suggest he lie down in the bedroom. Have a cool or warm drink ready for him. Arrange his pillow and offer to take his shoes. Speak in a soft, soothing and pleasant voice. Allow him to relax and unwind.

Listen to him. You may have a dozen things to tell him, but the moment of his arrival is not the time. Let him talk first.

Make the evening his. Never complain if he does not take you out to dinner or other places of entertainment. Instead, try to understand his world of strain and pressure, his need to be home and relax.

Your goal: Try to make your home a place of peace and order where your husband can renew himself in body and spirit.

Who wouldn't love one of those wives? But I'm not sure this mythical creature ever existed, except in textbooks or on celluloid. Without the "good wife" creating an island of tranquillity, our home was more like the Bermuda Triangle. We struggled like all parents working outside the home to shed our professional concerns on the porch as we entered the house. Physical presence alone will not suffice for children. We wanted to inspire their creativity, give them hope, engage in their celebrations.

It's been documented that children who do well in school have dinner with their families almost every night. My rules for my colleagues were: You can have me for breakfast and lunch, but you don't get dinner. The Schroeders often ate together in the House dining room when Congress went late, food fights and all. It was usually better than anything I could make. Only our dog got excited when I pulled out the pots and pans. Early on my children thought a balanced meal was holding a hamburger with both hands. I learned not to ask Jim to take me someplace on vacation I hadn't been, for he'd suggest the kitchen. But family dinner is about companionship and touching base, not the perfect pot roast. We survived just fine.

Raising children in a political arena was really charting new waters. I learned early on that if the kids were going to share the public spotlight with me, it had better be on their terms or it meant disaster. Right after I was elected to Congress, we had a huge Christmas eggnog party to thank supporters. Jamie, a very precocious age two, announced that she was not going. I accepted the challenge, stuffed her into a beautiful velvet dress, brushed her shining ringlets and told her she had to be there only a few minutes. Then grandparents would rescue her. Pouting all the way to the hall, she brightened as she saw the crowd, a huge crush of people. (After I won, suddenly everyone in Denver thought they'd worked on my campaign, and many of them wanted jobs.) The press rushed up to Jamie and asked the first question adults seem to always ask a child: "What do you want to be when you grow up?" Planting her patent-leathered feet on the floor, batting her eyes and projecting her voice so that nobody in the hall would miss her words, she said, "I want to be a congresswoman like my mother so I can say 'fuck' and 'shit' and not get in trouble." Then she looked at me, smiled and said, "I told you I didn't want to come."

I learned *never* to mandate appearances. Children always pay you back.

Political correctness is not part of a child's universe. Once, during the Carter administration, I took Jamie to a White House party. "This is the third time you've served brownies with nuts in them," she said to Rosalynn Carter, "and we told you we don't like nuts in our brownies." I was tempted to say, "Who do these children belong to?" and head for another corner of the room. When I sometimes showed up with Scott or Jamie, people often acted as if I'd worn a bathing suit to church. If I brought one of the kids to some public appearance where no one had anticipated a child's presence, people would point and ask, "What's that?" I'd answer, "A child—what did you think it was?"

Early in my first term, President Nixon invited us to a church service in the White House with Billy Graham. Graham had draped a religious cover over Nixon's presidency during Watergate, and I was not a fan of his. Nixon had said he couldn't go to church for security reasons, so Graham was conducting services in the White House. This made Nixon look like a beleaguered holy man. Nevertheless, I felt that respect for the office of the presidency required my attendance when Nixon invited us. It never occurred to me that children were not included. In our household, church was family time. When we showed up at the White House gate, there was a lot of huffing and puffing about my brazen attempt to crash the scene, and we were turned away. Twenty-three years later, Congress voted to give a special gold medal to Billy Graham. I was the only "No" vote in the House. I apologize, but I'm petty: I just couldn't get over those political church gatherings in the Nixon White House.

Just after I arrived in Congress, President Nixon vetoed a large day-care bill, and Congress couldn't override the veto. I thought any reasonable person would understand that subsidizing a parent's day care was more cost-effective than subsidizing a nonworking welfare family. Yet Nixon couldn't figure that out. Many people seemed to think that child care was a Communist plot. Trying to get my colleagues to pay attention, I organized Working Mother's Day in Congress on April 11, 1973. We encouraged members and their staff to bring children to the Hill and asked sympathetic workers without young children to wear a daisy in support. My Armed Services seatmate Ron Dellums and I were the only members of Congress to bring our children. It wasn't considered "professional." America was not ready for work and family issues. If you had a family, it was your problem, period.

Congress now has a day-care center, but it has been in jeopardy in the Republican Congress. Congress owns several buildings near the Capitol—parking garages, dorms for pages—and the day-care center was housed in one of those structures. But "privatization" became a buzzword among Newt Gingrich and his cronies, and the day-care center was the first thing they tried to sell in the name of privatization. They gave up only when everybody coughed and choked and said, "What are we going to tell the new owners: 'The building is yours, but it must be reserved for children?'" We've now progressed to the point where many members of Congress bring their children to work, but most of their staff aren't allowed the same privilege. I cheered when former representative Susan Molinari (Republican from New York) gave a speech saying, "Every time the word 'breastfeeding' is mentioned, there's a snicker on the House floor. This has been happening since the dawn of creation. Can we finally get a grip on it?" Newt Gingrich did help Susan and other new moms by providing a room for breastfeeding near the House floor.

One reason progress is so slow is that most elected members have traditional families with those "good wives" held up as paragons in my fifties home ec course. But only about 10 percent of America's families share the socioeconomic lifestyle of members of Congress. When someone says "day care," the men in Congress hear "baby-sitting." They don't understand that day care is not a luxury for working people. When many elected officials refuse to support better day care, family medical leave or tax breaks for dual-income families, my gut feeling is that they fear their "good wives" would run to join the workforce if society made it easier for them to deal with their caregiver roles. Obviously I can't prove this, but what else could make them vote no? They

talk like they're pro-family. I guess what they mean is everyone should just get a family like theirs—then there would be
no need for legislation!

When Jamie was born and I spent so many weeks in the
hospital, Jim had the same terrifying nightmare over and
over: He dreamt he got to work but could not go inside
because the children were in the car. "Congratulations," I
said, "you've just become a woman." As women do more outside the house, there is always tension about how many more
duties fathers assume. Jim is a loving and concerned father,
but soon after I was elected, I was reading an interview in
which Jim was asked how my election had changed his life.
His answer was, "I spend more time involved in things like
taking the children to the pediatrician." I immediately ran to
the House cloakroom and called him. "For five hundred dollars," I asked him, "what is the name of the children's pediatrician?" Knowing he was busted, he coughed and said, "Oh,
I was misquoted. I meant I *would* take them to the pediatrician if need be." The response to that interview was incredible. All sorts of women thought he hung the moon!

Jim was way ahead of his time, but he wasn't Mr. Mom.
Our family would have been shoeless, starving and wrinkled
if not for the services of some great housekeepers over the
years. But the legal status of our household help almost pro-
voked a crisis when the kids were little. Long before "Nan-
nygate," I knew it was important to dot every "i" and cross
every "t" in the paperwork for anyone I employed. Once I

got a call from the Immigration and Naturalization Service, stating that a background check on our housekeeper revealed she had not been living where we thought. It turned out to be a translation problem—her former employer in Japan did not speak English—and I was spared any embarrassment, but it turned my hair prematurely gray.

I did have great neighbors in Virginia I could call on if my housekeeper collapsed. I never knew how to thank them, so I would send flowers. One day the florist asked why I was always sending flowers to women!

With the whole family living at a frantic pace, it was important to deal directly with one another, not wasting energy on fits of pique or anger. I'd leave Post-it notes saying, "My birthday is Friday—forgetting it could be hazardous to your health!" Lipstick or shaving cream messages on mirrors were equally effective. I was really out of it on pop and sports celebrities. Whenever I seriously disappointed my children it was about "cultural" issues. A friend who is a rock music promoter asked me to have lunch with some people who had a resolution in the House for aid to earthquake victims in Nicaragua. They were a pleasant, intelligent, articulate couple. She was exotically pretty, he was very pale. When I got home that day, I told Scott and Jamie I'd had lunch with Bianca and Mick Jagger. The screams of "MOTHER!" could be heard all the way to DuPont Circle. I won't recite the other incidents where "MOTHER" hung in the air in disbelief. Being a member of Congress doesn't mean you are not square. Besides, I told them, I represent a box-shaped state so I have to be this way!

When Jamie was nine, she was getting over the flu and came to the office with me so I could keep an eye on her. That day I got a call from the White House, asking me to testify before a hearing for the Conference on Families. Jamie overheard the conversation and said, "*I* should be the one to testify."

"They're not asking children," I said.

"Well, they should," she countered. "How can they have a conference on families in the International Year of the Child and not hear from kids?" Trying to appease her, I asked an assistant to call and see if there was a day when children could testify. There was not. That only magnified her anger. Finally I called back and got the White House to agree that Jamie could use my time. She was ecstatic and set about devising a questionnaire for her school. It was simple and amazingly focused. She reported the results in front of Congress wearing a favorite maroon corduroy dress. She had asked questions like: "What do you think of when you hear the word 'grandparent'?" (Most kids said "telephone" or "airplane.") Or "What do your parents talk about at dinner?" (Most kids said that their parents talked about people at work, people the kids didn't know.) One boy was ashamed because he told friends that his father drove a train, thinking that's what "engineer" meant. And lots of kids said, "Our parents come to school, but we don't know where they go every day."

There was wonderful fallout from the survey. Many employers were inspired to hold Family Days at work. *Redbook* magazine gave Jamie an award for her gutsy presentation. She said it was stressful dealing with so many high-powered adults but worth it. A few weeks later, the two of us went into a shoe store, and a clerk said, "How nice to have a star with us!" I thought she meant me and said thank you. "Actually," she said, "I meant your daughter."

My young upstart also accompanied me to a Sunday evening dinner at a Denver synagogue where I was to talk about different issues in Congress. As we neared the temple, I saw helicopters in the air and knew there was some trouble. The Ku Klux Klan was out in force picketing in their dress whites. A police officer came to our car and asked that I use the back entrance. *No way*, I said to myself, *those thugs are not going to keep me from using the front door*. But looking at my daughter, my protective instincts took over. Quickly I came up with a solution.

"Jamie," I said, "you stay in the car with the nice police officer while Mom goes in. In a few minutes the TV cameras will leave and everyone will clear out. Then you and the officer can join me."

"Mother," Jamie said, firmly shutting the car door behind her, "Mrs. Roosevelt would roll over in her grave if she knew you told me to stay here."

"My God," said the cop, "you liberals ruin your children too." We plowed through the picket line with Jamie saying, "There are grown men in these sheets!" and the police officer running behind saying, "Shut that child up—I have to protect you."

Many years later Jamie and I ran into the Klan again. We had gone to Tampa, Florida, on a Sunday afternoon for a community march sponsored by local synagogues and churches after a series of horrible racial incidents, including one in which a young African American had been burned. Klan members in hooded white sheets were lining the streets—some of them whole families: Papa, Mama and Baby Bear Klansmen—taunting "Shame, shame," or "You're a traitor," or "Americans for America." Others wearing combat suits would run out into the street, stick video-cameras in our faces and threaten, "We're going to get you." To drown them out, one of the marchers started prancing and chanting in a high falsetto: "Hey, hey, watch the news, you'll see your dress doesn't match your shoes." Soon the cacophony of laughing voices had infuriated the Klan and all but obliterated their ugliness. Even with their pointed white cowls, they were unmasked, and an idiot unmasked is one of my favorite things.

When the kids went to college, Jim and I were reduced to the economics of our law school days, hoping we weren't in a car wreck because of the decrepit state of our underwear. We offered to buy Scott and Jamie T-shirts reading "This child is a Mercedes equivalent." Until they were out of college, I was terrified to talk about my modern child-rearing philosophy, afraid everything might blow up in my face. If the children got in trouble, it would be all my fault. I didn't want to look foolish for bragging about how well we juggled it all.

Here's how they turned out: Scott graduated from the foreign service school of Georgetown University; worked for the U.S.I.A. at a world expo in Brisbane, Australia; spent a year at ABC News; spent another year as a paralegal at a law firm, where he decided he didn't want to be a lawyer; got an MBA at Columbia Business School; and is now working for American Express. Somehow or other, I raised a capitalist tool living in America's largest toolbox, New York City. He is now engaged to a wonderful young woman, Amy Doel, of Sikh heritage. So I hope we'll soon have a great new daughter-in-law and bring some diversity into the family.

Jamie went to Princeton, majoring in Chinese, and then taught for a year at the University of Dalian, in northern China. True to her outspoken self, she was running her own little Tiananmen Square revolution—showing movies she wasn't supposed to show, assigning books the students weren't supposed to read, pushing the envelope of what the Chinese called "spiritual pollution." The military police in charge of that region would send an order that any student who donated blood would be excused from their midterm, and Jamie would respond, "It would be very nice for them to give blood, but I'm the teacher, and they are *not* excused from the test." Or the local prefect would declare that any student who helped to harvest the cabbages would be excused from class for a week, and Jamie would say, "They can harvest all the cabbages they want, but they have to make up their schoolwork."

She went all through China, to Manchuria and Tibet. A friend from Princeton who traveled with her, a young Chinese-American woman, felt even more pressure than Jamie. While local people called Jamie a word that translated as "big nose," they acted as if her friend descended from some lowly Chinese who were dumb enough to leave the motherland. Together the women were a traveling novelty act—Dalian wasn't like Beijing, which has Dunkin' Donuts and McDonald's. They often encountered some unpleasant, even hostile behavior. But Jamie found a clever method of protection: She got an eight-millimeter video-camera, and if she encountered any guff, she'd whip it out and say in perfect Chinese, "Do that again for the police." A ballsy act. Boy, I was glad when she came home.

It's hard to see your genes reincarnated in your children. You cheer and cry simultaneously. Jamie decided to get a master's degree in education at Cambridge University and is now studying for her Ph.D., eventually hoping to work in educational television. But she spent a summer training dolphins in Hawaii and sadly says she *knows* she'll never have a job that good again! Jim was also thrilled with that line of work. He used to say, "She can't marry a dolphin, and she can't bring one home, so how bad can it be?"

6

Enemy Camping

Out in Colorado, we like to say that you know a person by his enemies. I have quite a list and it's a source of great pride. In between the frustrations and stalemates of public life, there were times that I was able to crack the crusty old congressional culture with humor, employing the time-honored tradition of "gotcha" politics. These moments were glorious.

On one of those occasions, the navy had asked me down to Pensacola, Florida, to meet with the first class of women to be trained as aviators. I was thrilled: I'd never been included in such "guy" things. As a pilot myself, I was a strong advocate of women moving into these roles. It was Mother's Day weekend, so my whole family accompanied me to Florida. That afternoon, back at the hotel, we were changing into beach clothes when a young naval officer, sweating profusely in his white uniform, appeared at the door.

"Ma'am," he said, "you are hereby ordered to accompany me to a fund-raiser for Congressman Robert Sikes." Sikes was a Florida Democrat from Hébert's branch of the party. We were ideological opposites and always at each other's throats. I couldn't figure out why he would want me there.

"I don't think so," I said.

The officer got a pained look on his face. "Ma'am," he said, "if I don't bring you to this event, it could mean the end of my navy career." Bob Sikes chaired the Defense Appropriations Subcommittee, and when he said "Jump," the military asked, "How high?"

My husband had been in the navy and had great sympathy for the young officer ordered to deliver me. "Sikes wants to show his power to the locals," Jim said. "He wants them to see that he can deliver all these elected officials to honor him. You've got to go."

Furious, I changed my bathing suit for a business suit that was just as uncomfortable as the officer's uniform and drove with him to a barbecue set up on the grounds of a local school. Sikes was seated on an outdoor stage surrounded by thousands of people, many of whom were lined up to place gifts in front of him, like Yul Brynner in *The King and I*. Sikes referred to himself as a "he-coon," and many of the gifts were raccoons in cages. Someone explained to me that she-coons are the bitchiest, snarliest critters in the forest, and he-coons can conquer them. Sikes clearly thought he was a studly dude. I bet he secretly thought I was a she-coon!

Suddenly the Boy Scouts who were directing traffic cleared a path, and into the school yard came a phalanx of perhaps fifty Alabama state policemen on motorcycles and in patrol cars. At the center of this grandiose escort group was the governor of Alabama, George Wallace.

I was the only woman in the group — not even a female raccoon to back me up. Sikes insisted that I speak. So I took the microphone, smiling sweetly. Remembering my sister raccoons I said: "I'm sure everyone is surprised to see me here honoring Bob Sikes because most people know we disagree on many issues. But I took time out of my Mother's Day weekend to be here so that Bob's constituents would all know what a fantastic help he has been in trying to get the Equal Rights Amendment passed, and how hard he has worked to keep abortions safe and legal." The crowd started murmuring. Sikes looked as if he was going to throw up, but I didn't stop. "Florida is one of the states that has not ratified the ERA," I said, "and I wonder if that's because the local press here has been so negligent in reporting what leaders like Bob Sikes *really think* about it. So thanks, Bob, for standing up with the congresswomen, and now I'm off to rejoin my family on the beach." The she-coon beat the he-coon that day: No one asked me to stay.

Sometimes "gotcha" politics even had its use with

friends. Tip O'Neill was a huge, huggable teddy bear who didn't have a mean bone in his body, but he always introduced me at political gatherings in a different way than he introduced my male colleagues. He didn't understand when I tried to explain my objections. Finally I got my chance to introduce him to a group working on getting an extension for ERA. "I'm honored to present Millie O'Neill's husband," I told the crowd. "We've always marveled at how Tip has been able to combine career and family. Of course, we all know that the most important thing in his life is his four children." When I looked over at Tip, the color was draining from his face. I knew he "got" my message for the first time. I was forgiven, but the lesson wasn't forgotten. That was the best thing about Tip: He wasn't mired in cement or locked into ideology. He could process new information and adjust. He'd been a big supporter of U.S. involvement in Vietnam, until a group of nuns came to his office and changed his mind. When the House finally voted on the Equal Rights Amendment, Tip said that he looked up into the gallery to see his wife and daughters, and realized he was voting for his own family.

Fighting for passage of the Equal Rights Amendment, I sometimes felt too personally involved and often lost sight of my own counsel to keep a sense of humor. On a freezing evening in December 1979, I joined many others for a vigil outside the Oakton Church of Latter Day Saints in suburban Virginia where a Mormon council was putting Sonia Johnson on trial. Sonia had been a pillar of her religious community and the church organist. Now she was threatened with excommunication over her support of ERA. As we huddled outside in the cold, there was a prayer service and rally sponsored by Religious Advocates for Equality. Supporters included many men from a group called M.A.N. for ERA. There were even members of the Redskins football team present. Sonia had to enter the building through the back door, and her husband, Richard, was forbidden to accompany her. It felt like I was at the Salem witch trials three hundred years ago. One hour passed, two hours, three hours. We got colder and colder. After four hours, she was excommunicated. I was despondent and knew of no way to respond but to work harder for women's rights.

When I arrived in Congress, there were no women working as pages, Capitol police, doorkeepers or parliamentarians. Congress had passed laws about sex discrimination but conveniently exempted itself. It was a cross between a plantation and a fraternity house—the former being the public persona and the latter its private moments. In one charming episode, Representative Otto Passman (Democrat from Louisiana) decided to train a woman on his staff, Shirley Davis, to become his administrative assistant. Six months later he fired her and wrote her a letter saying, "On account of the unusually heavy workload, I concluded that it was essential that the under-study to my administrative assistant be a man." If any employer in the private sector had written that letter, it would be a prima facie violation of federal laws against sex discrimination. Passman voted for those laws, but as a congressman he was exempted from obeying them. Shirley Davis sued. I was the only member of Congress to stand up for her. Crossing the line between congressional member and staff was a huge violation of the institution's unwritten rules. Passman developed a full-body twitch—people joked that he was wearing his suits out from the inside—and some people blamed me. Finally Shirley Davis won her suit, but it was a Pyrrhic victory: No damages were allowed under House rules. Since this episode, the rules have been changed to provide back pay, reinstatement, even monetary damages for this kind of discrimination. My raising money to help her with legal costs and supporting her case caused many colleagues to shun me forever.

The congressional legislative pattern is to pass a sweeping bill and then write regulations that exempt Congress. The press exposes the exemption, Congress feigns shock, and the process starts again. The only good I can see in this cycle is that it provides full employment for investigative reporters.

In the 1970s, right after Congressman Wayne Hays (Democrat from Ohio) was caught with his girlfriend, I was joined by Mo Udall and Charlie Rose in creating a House Fair Employment Practices Bill that put the plantation under the same federal rules we passed for everyone else. Senator John Glenn (Democrat from Ohio) pushed it in the Senate. But every single year, both houses of Congress would find a clandestine way to strangle the bill. For years they got away with saying: There are three separate branches of government, and we'd love to have the Equal Employment Opportunity Commission or the Civil Rights Commission monitor us, but it would be unconstitutional.

Knowing that the bill was not a top priority with my colleagues and that we might not live long enough to see it passed, the three of us joined to set up a voluntary Fair Employment Practices group. About one hundred members signed the agreement. We policed ourselves through a board composed fifty-fifty of members of Congress and their staff. The board made sure we practiced what we legislated. This end run around the legislative process made the leadership furious. They refused to give us office space or even put our phone number and address in the Capitol directories. Congresswoman Lynn Martin (Republican from Illinois) joined me in the cause. Finally, we shamed the House into passing a modified bill. But then they hid the enforcement agency in the office of the House doorkeeper. The person holding that job is elected by and owes allegiance to the very members of Congress who might be charged with unfair practices. Anyone who found the office and filed a claim was subjected to psychiatric investigation. ("Have you been having headaches, Miss Smith?") So we kept pushing. "Incremental" is the best description for the progress Congress is making policing itself.

I don't think that Congress quite understood how much it was perceived as an overaged frat house until the Clarence Thomas hearings in 1991. At the start of the hearings to confirm him as Supreme Court Justice, the House was out of session over a holiday weekend. I had heard that a young African-American woman named Anita Hill had approached the Judiciary Committee alleging sexual harrassment by Thomas and asking to testify, but the committee had said no. By the time I returned to my office, we were logging dozens of calls from women all over the country, outraged that Hill was being denied the right to speak.

A group of congresswomen decided to talk with Senator George Mitchell (Democrat of Maine), the majority leader. I called to ask for an appointment and was told, "He's busy having his regular Democratic luncheon." I said, "We're Democrats, too, and we've got a disaster in the making." Together with Patsy Mink, Barbara Boxer and half a dozen other Democratic congresswomen, I walked over to the Senate office building, trailed by the media. It was a trip of about three hundred feet, but you would have thought we had marched across the Kalahari Desert.

When I knocked on the door of the dining room, one of Mitchell's staffers peeked out and said, "We don't let strangers in here."

I had had enough. "You go tell George that half the Washington press corps is fifty feet away," I said quietly. A few minutes later Mitchell came out and took us down to his office for a meeting, where we convinced him to intervene with Senator Joe Biden (Democrat from Delaware), the chairman of the Senate Judiciary Committee. Apparently Senator John Danforth (Republican from Missouri), Thomas's friend and mentor, had been assured that confirmation of Thomas would be a slam dunk—swift and perfunctory.

The committee was apologetic in its acquiescence to the demand that Hill be heard, something along the lines of, "We don't want this any more than he does—it's just that wacky Constitution." I think the committee members were feeling some white guilt: They saw a black face and were terrified of raising any untoward, unseemly issues. Anita Hill's was a black face, too, just a less important female one. She was granted permission to tell her story, to be interrogated, ridiculed, vilified.

But the good news was: That's how we got all those

new women elected to Congress in 1992. We went from 5 percent to 10 percent, which doesn't sound like much representation for 51 percent of the population, but it was important. Women were outraged at the way Hill had been treated by the boys' club (parodied on an episode of *Murphy Brown*, with an actor bearing a remarkable resemblance to Senator Howell Heflin from Alabama harrumphing in a Southern drawl, and a Ted Kennedy–esque senator commenting on the attractiveness of witnesses). Barbara Boxer was elected senator from California, and perhaps her single most distinctive campaign image was that photograph of us marching to Mitchell's office. It's interesting that the conventional wisdom is that Schroeder went to the mat for "her good friend" Anita Hill. I had never even met the woman then, though I admired her guts and still do.

Another congressional no-no I took on was federal pensions. Each branch of government has its own pension system: There are military pensions, foreign service pensions, judicial, civil service and, yes, congressional pensions. Laws governing divorce and family property are determined by state laws. Everyone was shocked when the Supreme Court held that federal pensions were not marital property but delayed salary, and therefore above state law. In other words, pensions remained with the federally employed spouse who "earned" them. (Of course justices are above the taint of a conflict of interest, despite the fact that they have federal pensions themselves.) The decision startled family law specialists, and many divorcing women found themselves beached and penniless. I couldn't figure out why working for the government should allow someone the special right to shed their economic responsibility for their family like a snake sheds a skin. I believed real "family values" should apply to the government too. So I went to work to have federal pensions treated like private pensions. Surprise—this did not meet with a good reception from my colleagues. (The cynical side of me wants to point out the high rate of congressional divorces as a possible motivation.) My advocacy got me a brick thrown through my car window in our Virginia suburb, where there were plenty of neighbors who worked at the Pentagon. And I had the opportunity to meet sheriffs in many different cities where there were nasty demonstrations, mostly by retired military men incensed over pension-sharing. My pension legislation generated more enemies than almost anything else I've done. It also generated more friends—ex-wives who didn't have to go on welfare or food stamps.

In 1996, my last year in office, Congressman Robert Dornan (Republican from California) tried to undo a provision that I'd passed thirteen years earlier. It allowed a divorce court the right to order sharing military pensions with a spouse. He wanted to make the change retroactive and have wives pay the money back. It was an election year. I pointed out to the Armed Services Committee that if the members wanted to start all-out gender wars, this would be a real opening volley. We stopped Dornan's proposal, and the voters stopped Dornan—he was defeated later that year by a young Hispanic woman named Loretta Sanchez. Nevertheless, I predict vigilance is still needed.

I never made Nixon's enemies list, but Oliver North named me one of the twenty-five most dangerous people in America. I like to imagine this brave marine sleeping with a night-light because I'm on the prowl. Somebody from the Christian Coalition called me "a witch, a snake and a whore" in a Denver newspaper. The Republican National Committee printed a "Most Wanted" poster including my picture to scare people into sending money to fight demonic Democrats. A magazine called *Soldier of Fortune*, printed in Boulder, called me "comrade" and went after me because I did not fall down and worship guns. (In the Rocky Mountains I would have done so much better politically if I had embraced the Second Amendment and forgotten about the First.)

Sadly, I made enemies out of some constituents. Once

a big box was delivered containing a sculpture: a tree with an effigy of me hanging from a noose. Another time the Denver police picked up a man who turned out to have a room full of firearms and the plans to my house. Then there was the rally when my campaign manager, Larry Wright, saw a man who looked familiar standing at the back of an auditorium.

"You've been to several of Pat's speeches, haven't you?" Larry asked enthusiastically.

"Yeah," the man replied, "and one day I'm going to try and shoot the bitch."

I didn't tell my family about these incidents; I didn't take them too seriously—as an expression we have out west goes, I figured most of these guys were all hat and no cattle. Colorado seems to attract folks with great passion for their cause. It's the home of the arch-conservative Promise Keepers and a number of antigovernment militia groups. And it's where a liberal radio talk-show host named Alan Berg was shot to death. Such a tradition was enough to spook me if I dwelled on it. One night I was at home alone and heard a noise in the basement. Unmistakable: Someone was down there. Terrified, I crept to the cellar door and peered down, to see two teenaged boys, friends of Jamie's, who had crawled in through the doggy door and were hanging beer cans on the fake elkhead over the fireplace. I owe quite a few of my gray hairs to that incident.

I never thought of my opponents from a dozen different political races as enemies, but they thought I was one. I was accused of being pro-Communist, antigun, soft on defense, hardline on busing. Sometimes the claims were so weird, I was left with my mouth agape. One opponent said that I was born in Wisconsin and was a tool of the cheese industry. (Nobody in my family had ever been to that state. And just what would the cheese lobby want, anyway?) Another claimed, "This Schroeder woman is so crazy, she voted to send rockets to Czechoslovakia." We looked that one up. There had been an international toy fair in Prague, during the Cold War. Congress had to vote to allow American manufacturers to send items behind the Iron Curtain. Yes, I voted to allow Mattel Toys to send Nerf rockets to the toy fair!

The election issues seemed to get more puerile as my own campaigning became more sophisticated. In my second campaign I was proud and happy to upgrade from the dilapidated old drugstore headquarters. Our new digs were in the Carr building in downtown Denver. It was built by the Buddhist Society as housing for Japanese senior citizens and named for the courageous governor of Colorado during World War II. He had refused to build internment camps for Japanese-Americans in his state and lost his reelection. (Our next-door neighbors when I was growing up were interned during the war, and I wrote my college thesis on the camps.) Governor Carr had been the type of leader I wanted to be.

One of my female opponents in a minor party wanted to make it illegal for women to wear nylons—if I'd really been out there working for women, she argued, I would recognize that nylons were the symbol of women's oppression. Actually, she might have a point. I just had a few other issues to deal with first.

I ran against Republican women in five out of twelve races. One of the antichoice male candidates not only called me a baby-killer but would vigorously start chopping his hand up and down to demonstrate his claim that I was chopping up the livers of unborn children. Another opponent literally dragged a wooden soapbox around town, saying we were going to debate on street corners. She wouldn't bother to tell me the location and then would start yelling and flapping her arms when I didn't show up.

In 1984 my opponent was a woman who belonged to the Daughters of the American Revolution and wore a fur stole that looked like roadkill. Her bone of contention was that I had given a speech against mandating school prayer, invoking a hilarious comedy routine by Mark Russell. Mark tried to write a national prayer along the lines of "Give us this day our daily bread . . ." that would include every segment of the population by the kind of bread they ate (bagel, tortilla, nan, you get the idea). Obviously I was the Antichrist—otherwise how could I make fun of prayer? In 1990 my opponent was Gloria Gonzales Romer, a Hispanic woman who had married a man from a wealthy oil family and moved into the Polo Grounds, the most elite section of town. At least she was honest. She often gave speeches to youth about the importance of marrying well and good connections like the Junior League. She also had the best wardrobe of any opponent I had.

It's easy to get on the ballot in Colorado. There was a time when it was hard to keep track of all the political parties: the Labor Party (who wanted me to admit I was a patsy for Nelson Rockefeller), the Tea Party (who didn't want to pay taxes), the Sky Pilots Party (I can't remember what they wanted—blue skies?). The one thing they all wanted was to be on the televised debates, so everybody would end up with two minutes' time. They do have a right to run, but it creates a lot of clutter, noise, and confusion. TV stations were delighted to no longer have regulations about community service so they could drop these debates. Now it's mainly ads voters see. I think if parties representing more than 10 percent of the vote were given debate time, we'd be better off.

In 1992 I ran against a man who had been an intern in my office. Midway through the campaign, he stated he was bisexual. The poor guy was going around town with paper plates showing how people could make yard signs for him. That election was rather a freebie.

My toughest campaign was probably back in 1978, when my first opponent, Arch Decker, ran again. This time he was a Republican. But I really ran against Craig Morton, the handsome former quarterback for the Denver Broncos, who was his campaign manager. Because Craig was so popular, Decker joined himself at the hip to the popular jock, and people were dazzled by the celebrity factor. I won again, but my minister almost conceded that race. "You can run against God," he said, "but I don't know about football."

No enemy energized me quite like Phyllis Schlafly, the "über-housewife" who made her reputation fighting the Equal Rights Amendment, although she was a lawyer who ran for Congress and got miffed because Ronald Reagan didn't make her secretary of defense. Despite my limited time in the kitchen, I'll bet I cooked more meals at home than she did. Schlafly was the sort of woman who wrapped herself in "family values" but didn't support her own son when she found out he was gay. Once she insisted on having her seat changed at a Washington restaurant when she realized that I was at the next table. Is feminism contagious?

Schlafly always looked like she came out of a Talbots catalogue from 1952. The anti-ERA forces must have had a dress code; they all wore nearly identical pastels and ruffles, conjuring up images of those perfect housewives Hollywood portrayed in Doris Day movies. But Schlafly was the worst of the bunch. One of my constitutional law professors who found himself quoted by Schlafly in her speeches wrote to warn her to stop using his name and words out of context. She never did. She distorted so sweetly! We debated several times on national television, but she was so fraudulent and misleading, I finally said I'd only debate somebody who was elected, not self-appointed. That ruined her game, for no matter how many times she ran she never could get herself elected. She could be one hundred miles away from the truth and it doesn't matter if it's just talk. If you're accountable to voters, you're more responsible about what you say.

It was depressing that while I was pushing hard for women's rights, the first to criticize my agenda were often other women. Opportunity for all women has been a hard sell. Women in government who have the power to come onboard often refuse to lend their support unless the issue strikes a personal chord. When we wanted to open the military academic doors to women, some women responded, "Who wants to go to a military academy?" When I was working on breast cancer legislation, I'd hear, "My sister has lupus, and I want funding for that." Other minority communities are much better at rallying politically around generic betterment for all. They understand that more opportunity is good for everyone, even if it's seemingly irrelevant to their own personal lives.

Study after study shows that women make a real difference when they finally become a critical mass in any institution, a critical mass being somewhere between 35 and 40 percent. Congress is a long way from critical mass. More than two hundred years ago we fought against taxation without representation, but our own government hasn't caught on. Women and men pay taxes equally even though female business owners get only 2 percent of federal contracts. There are all sorts of government programs women pay for equally but don't play in equally. Nobody has cottoned to my "modest proposal" to correct this imbalance: The men don't have to share the business, but we cut women's federal taxes. If women get 2 percent of federal programs and contracts, we only pay 2 percent of the cost. This is a solution rooted in our traditions. But to Congress—NO SALE.

The 1992 election brought a flood of women to the polls and a dynamic group of new women into government. They passed historic legislation. President Clinton signed these bills into law: laws about family leave, health equity, domestic violence, repeal of the gag rule for abortions. In 1994 many of those new congresswomen were defeated, and the exit polls showed why: Women who voted in 1992 didn't bother in 1994. Such fickleness doesn't play well in politics. We have to be serious full-time players. And we have to play hardball.

Here's what I mean by hardball. Traditionally, politicians' wives have always been sent out to address various groups of female constituents. But I couldn't send my husband to address a group of men. Men understand power and won't accept a spouse as a substitute for the policymaker. I was the one with the vote on the House floor, and the men wanted a direct shot at me. They're right, and women should demand the same thing. Until we do, we will be seriously marginalized.

When I was pushing family legislation, male colleagues often said to me, "No one ever mentions day care, pay equity, family leave or women's health to *me*." That's because their wives represented them at the meetings where those were the main topics. When women lobby, we have to think like Exxon would think. Demand direct access to the policy-makers, not an eighteen-year-old intern substitute. If an elected representative refuses to meet women to discuss their agenda, they should write to newspapers asking other citizens if they have any suggestions about breaking through, or print up fliers with the legislator's photo asking: "Has anyone seen this person?" Have fun with it. Use your power. Make your representatives deal with you.

In one of the classic cases of misdirected passion, a group of working mothers had raised enough money through bake sales to hire several buses and come to Washington with their children, to meet with the women in Congress about the need for better day care in the workplace. They wanted to talk with people they perceived as their friends, but they were preaching to the choir. "Our consciousness is raised," I told them. "Why don't you go down the hall to the offices of the congressmen who've shown no support for day-care legislation and drop off your kids? Let them baby-sit for a few hours—give them a taste of caring for children." Politicians were always out having well-orchestrated "work days"—pumping gas, raking lawns, getting their hands dirty—but I don't know any man who rolled up his sleeves in a day-care center. It's interesting what our male colleagues think of as work.

Individuals may have less leverage than groups, but they've still got a voice and options. I've always thought that the tradition of writing a letter to your congressman is a pretty meager idea; what goes on between one government official and one constituent doesn't pack much of a wallop. How much more effective to make a poster that says: "WANTED: Pat Schroeder. This creep does x, y or z." Then mail it to me with a note that says, "I just made one thousand of these, and I think I'll put them in menus wherever I eat, and elevators, and restrooms, and bus shelters, and the laundromat. . . ." *Now* you have my attention. Even without critical mass, women can wield power.

7

The Presidential Weep-Stakes

In the spring of 1987, I was cochairing the presidential campaign of my fellow Coloradan Gary Hart. Gary and I had been young attorneys together in Denver and in many ways had parallel lives. We lived in the same part of town, knew the same people, and he was spearheading the McGovern campaign in 1972 when I first ran for Congress. In 1974 when he campaigned for the Senate, a lot of my supporters worked for him. Upon his election, he went on the Armed Services Committee of the Senate while I was on that committee in the House. When Jim and I sold our house in Denver, we bought an apartment building and turned it into condominium units, one of which Gary and Lee Hart bought. The local papers had a few jokes over the idea that we were all living in the same place. "It isn't a *commune*," Lee Hart kept saying, "it's a *condo*."

Gary is a cipher. He didn't suffer fools lightly and didn't like small talk. He was certainly a engaging dinner guest, but not one to discuss whether the dinner should be Thai food or Italian, or what movie he'd seen the night before. He was into substance. He kept saying I was his good friend, and I thought: *If I'm his good friend, he has no good friends*. I felt comfortable with Gary, but never close. There was always a wall.

Gary is smart, but he's painfully shy, never seeming to enjoy people. In 1980 when he was running for reelection to the Senate, I organized a "Get Out the Vote" party at our condo pool. The polls showed he was in real trouble—in fact, he barely won—but he still stayed up in his apartment, refusing to come down and meet people. The schmoozing and glad-handing part of politics was sheer agony for him. I'd helped him with his presidential campaign in 1984, but in 1987 nobody knew if he was going to make a presidential run. I was preparing to join my husband on a business trip to Thailand with Jamie, as well as my college roommate, Betty Endicott. Betty was the first female TV news director in Washington, and she was bringing her daughter. As the time for me to leave got closer, I still couldn't get a straight answer from Gary's office: Was he going to announce or wasn't he? Did he want me to cochair his campaign or didn't he? I don't think his staff knew either. He was really conflicted.

Finally they said—go. I did, and when I got to Thailand and picked up a copy of the *International Herald Tribune*, there Gary was, standing all alone in the red rocks of the Colorado mountains, announcing his candidacy. In retrospect, the lonely imagery of this picture captured the race.

For several years there had been rumors about Gary's sexual peccadilloes. The buzz was uncomfortable for me—here I am, Ms. Feminist—and as cochair of his campaign, I didn't sit down and have a conversation with him at that level. But I knew how insidious gossip could be inside the Beltway. If a man traveled with a woman, people said, "*Hmmmmmm.*" It a woman traveled with a man, people said, "*Hmmmmmm.*" If a woman traveled with a woman, people said, "*Hmmmmmm, the husband's a beard.*" There's nothing you can do that's right. Washington thrives on gossip, and there was a certain tier of staff that got its credence (or thought it did) by supplying the press with morsels, all the way up to the White House. When Ronald Reagan first came to power, Diana McClellan, who wrote "The Ear" column for the *Washington Post*, ran an item that the Carters had bugged Blair House to find out what the Reagans were up to. The Carters went ballistic, threatened to sue, and the item was retracted.

One of Hart's staff, Mike Cheroutes, had run my office for my first two years in Congress, and he said, "There's nothing there. How could you even raise the question or repeat those ugly stories?" So I felt secure in backing Hart.

One day in May, the campaign called and asked if I could represent Gary at appointments with the editorial boards of newspapers in Ohio and California. I was often asked to fill in for him at what he considered to be "second-tier" events. This was more last minute than most requests, and I had to jettison my whole schedule to accommodate him. As soon as I checked into my California hotel room, the phone rang. It was Jim. "Don't answer any more calls!" he warned. "Everybody's looking for you! Turn on the TV. You won't believe what happened."

What had happened is, of course, an indelible part of American history. Defending himself against a reputation as a womanizer, Gary had boldly dared the press to "go ahead and follow me." Reporters for the *Miami Herald* did. Gary was discovered and photographed on a yacht in Bimini called *Monkey Business* with a blonde named Donna Rice on his lap. This was the pressing business that prevented his making the trip!

I have to admit that my first reaction was, "Do you mean I've been canceling my schedule, flying to these godforsaken places, eating pressed hamster or whatever that airplane food is, while he's on a pleasure boat in Florida?" The fallout came very quickly, and the Hart campaign self-destructed. I never even tendered a formal resignation as cochair and never actually had a conversation about it with Gary or with Lee, for whom I felt a great sadness. (Lee is the sister of Kansas Congresswoman Martha Keyes, and I always thought she had more political skills in dealing with people than Gary did.) Overnight it was a total meltdown.

Although Gary and I are still cordial when we meet, our friendship was history too. Perhaps he felt I didn't adequately "defend" him and was angry because I was not prepared to fall on my sword for him. I felt we'd all been let down by him. I felt he used me because having a woman at the head of his campaign might deflect these issues. But Donna Rice wasn't sitting in *my* lap, and I just didn't have the energy to even engage asking why she was in Gary's.

Part of the disappointment stemmed from my knowledge that Gary was in so many ways a feminist. He was always helpful at home, setting the table, doing the dishes or laundry, and it was natural—no big deal. On every women's issue raised in Congress, he was instinctively there. I guess if the retro types get in trouble with women, I'm not surprised, but my heart breaks when it's the good guys, like Hart, Kennedy and Robert Packwood. (Packwood was every Democratic woman's dream—*on the issues*. Gloria Steinem raised money for him!) I'm not sure why I have these different standards, but I keep hoping people will act as they vote, that their private lives will match their public personae. If they have a lousy voting record on women's issues, I don't expect much.

After Hart dropped out, friends and supporters began to urge me to take a look at the presidential race myself. That's all it was—a look. You were willing to do this for someone else, they said. Why not do it for yourself? "We've got all these candidates but no real choices," people said. "If nothing else, you can add something to the debate." Hart's supporters were grief-stricken—total believers who had not come out of mourning. It was so late to consider a run; everybody in Iowa and New Hampshire, where the early, important caucuses take place, had signed up for their candidates long before. In June, less than a month after Hart dropped out, my "look" exploded on the front page of the *New York Times* and the television news. (It was surely a "leak." I never seem to learn that there's always a trusted someone on staff who wants to win points with reporters.) I was on a plane headed to Denver and when I got off, the world was there. I never had to call a press conference.

The essential question I was looking at was, "Is America man enough to back a woman?" I set up headquarters in Jim's office. (He was with a law firm started by a couple of guys who had been in the Peace Corps, working on international trade issues.) Pam Solo, who had run several of my congressional races, agreed to chair my campaign. Kathy Bonk, who had been media director for the NOW Legal Defense Fund, quit her job to handle my press relations. I'd met Gary David Goldberg, who produced the TV show

Family Ties, and now *Spin City.* When I gave a speech in Richmond about television images of women, he became campaign treasurer. The seven other Democratic candidates had been running for months: Governors Michael Dukakis and Bruce Babbitt; Senators Paul Simon, Joe Biden and Al Gore; Representative Dick Gephardt and the Reverend Jesse Jackson. Almost overnight, I had to explore publicly the questions other candidates had considered much earlier and in private: Could I raise the necessary money, build an organization, be accepted? How would my message be different and how would I fine-tune it? Instantly, I was seen as Everywoman, advancing the female struggle for a stronger voice in government. Like it or not, my potential candidacy for the highest elected office in our country was going to be a hook for political pundits to appraise the progress of women.

I used scheduled airlines to travel and figured the first flight out in the morning was the most apt to be on time. There were a lot of early wakeup calls. Checking luggage meant losing time, so I struggled to find outfits that could be stuffed into carry-on bags and still look crisp. I was so jealous that the men could pack dark blue suits, white shirts and red ties, and emerge unscathed from a cross-country flight. What can a woman wear to appear presidential, especially in the summer when it's a struggle just not to look wilted? If I wore the same outfit on national news twice in a week, people would comment. "Pat

Schroeder couldn't be there because her plaid dress was at the cleaners."

Traveling around the country was like a series of rapid-fire blind dates. People I'd never seen before would meet me in each city, get me through the schedule and back to the airport on time. My congressional colleagues, for the most part, had endorsed Dick Gephardt. The Speaker of the House, Jim Wright, would hold meetings every Wednesday morning on the third floor of the Capitol to let the "whips" from each region of the country know what bills were coming up. He'd talk about what a great candidate Gephardt was. Occasionally a staffer would whisper in his ear that I was running too, but he'd dismiss it with a grunt. Congresswoman Nancy Pelosi (Democrat from California) came to a San Francisco fund-raiser, and Congresswoman Barbara Kennelly (Democrat from Connecticut) came to one in New England, but most of my colleagues reacted like Congressman Les Aspin, who kept asking if I had lost my mind.

I decided I would not make this a symbolic campaign. I would run only if I had a good chance to win. The press had categorized me as a "women's candidate." I didn't want to deny my gender, but I also did not want my gender to block my message. Many could not get beyond the fact I looked *so* different from the others. I also did not want to go heavily into debt. If, at the end of the summer, I didn't have enough campaign money to be competitive,

Seven congresswomen—Snowe, me, Boggs, Ferraro, Oakar, Mikulski, Byron—at NASA for Sally Ride's historic flight. She was the first American woman in space. Such pride we had in Sally Ride.

"O.K., Pat, I won't sing if you won't—Best Wishes"   *George Bush*

The annual House Gym Dinner with Congresswoman Marilyn Lloyd (Tennessee), Peter Rodino, and George Bush. As a kid, I was given movie money when I showed up for choir practice. Now the president asks me not to sing, also!

Jim and me with President Corazon Aquino in the Philippines. I really was in awe of her bravery, sincerity and openness. Note—she doesn't wear power suits!

Pakistani Prime Minister Benazir Bhutto, one of the few women on the international political scene. America may not be man enough to elect a woman, but Pakistan was.

Russian President Boris Yeltsin. You felt he was stuffed in his body and could pop out of it any moment!

Jiang Zemin, new head of China, in Beijing, 1993. He laughs his way around the world. Have you ever seen a serious picture of him?

British House Speaker Betty Boothroyd, with Tom Foley, then her American counterpart. She's the best! The House of Commons can make Congress look like the Boy Scouts, but she can handle them.

Senator Brock Adams (Washington) at one of many breast cancer rallies. Congresswoman Marilyn Boyd (Tennessee) said at one she'd get her mammogram that weekend. She let it slip and ended up having a mastectomy—but survived. Don't forget.

Speaking at a Violence Against Women Act (VAWA) rally. It was thrilling to have it pass as part of the Crime Bill, but after the Republicans won in 1994, they tried to defund it. It's an old political trick: Vote for it but don't fund it. With the help of Republican congresswomen, we held most of the funding.

A spontaneous rally on the Capitol grounds after the Tienanmen Square massacre. The Chinese students at local universities were stunned, as we all were, by the TV images coming from their homeland.

This was a camp of contra supporters in Nicaragua. What a quagmire that whole 1980s Central America mess was.

With Vice President Al Gore. My motto and modus operandi was "Never waste an opportunity to get a word in."

Joe Kennedy Jr., Bill Clinton, and me. The flag on the back of my clipboard was a protective shield against right-wingers.

Exchanging jerseys from our respective home universities with Rep. Virginia Smith of Nebraska. We were doing the "guy" thing of betting on our team's scores.

As the senior Democratic woman, I was one of four designated counters at the opening of each congressional session to certify the outcome of the speaker's election. That's me with Frank Annunzio (Illinois), Bill Frenzel (Minnesota), and Virginia Smith (Nebraska). Who says we can't count?

Bill Clinton signing the Women's Health Equity Act.

Bill Clinton arrives in Denver for a bill-signing. (Note—both of us are talking!)
Gary Hart is at the far right.

Hillary Rodham Clinton in
Denver for my health-care
forum. What a woman!

Campaigning in the '80s. I
never knew what to do
with corsages.

Washington, D.C., staff. We were trying to be cheerful during the Bush years and look like 1,000 points of light.

Outside the House chamber in the Speaker's Lobby after a State of the Union address with Bill Clinton and Al Gore. Members all firehose them with facts every chance we get. The amazing thing is Clinton and Gore absorb them.

With Lindy Boggs and Nancy Johnson (Connecticut) at Lindy's photo portrait unveiling. Just before this picture was taken, a young child visiting the Capitol ran up to me *so* excited and said, "I didn't know Disney did dresses for adults."

Dr. T. Berry Brazelton was a terrific supporter of the Family Medical Leave Act. He went on our Great American Family Tour, came to Washington and Denver and I want him for president. Imagine a pediatrician in the Oval Office.

With Henry Kissinger. Think of the captions this could generate—like,
"No kidding, Pat, what do you really do?"

Marilyn Bergman, songwriter, and Barbra Streisand on Capitol Hill.
She is butter!

I thanked the Queen for coming to Congress because we finally got the Congressional Women's Lounge redecorated. She thought that was funny, but it was the truth!

I received an award from the New York ACLU with Harry Belafonte in June 1997. What a *hunk* he is!

John Kennedy Jr. at a party thrown by *George*, the magazine he founded. When he visited me in my D.C. office, he was interested in a photo I had of his dad with Harry Truman. When he got married, I sent it to him as a gift and got the nicest letter back. He said it is very difficult to have the name of a father everyone knew and he didn't. My heart goes out to him.

Greeting a young constituent.

This young constituent won a speech-giving contest. He said he wanted a profession where he could make money by talking, so he came to visit me.

With Kwasi Mfume on a congressional trip to South Africa before the election of Nelson Mandela.

My seatmate Ron Dellums and Roscoe Dellums.

My brother Mike, far right, my parents, next right, and friends crashing my induction into the Women's Hall of Fame in Seneca Falls, New York, 1996.

Jamie's graduation from Princeton, 1992. We had to tether Jim (class of '58) so he didn't float away.

Hawaii vacation, 1996.

THAT'S GOING TO BE ONE AWFULLY BIG MOUTH TO FILL.

°PAT SCHROEDER°

This appeared in the *Rocky Mountain News* shortly after I announced my retirement.

At a campaign stop. Yes, I love this country. Had I been born in another time or country, I'd probably be dead or in jail.

I said I'd pull the plug. David Brinkley reduced this message to a television sound bite, "No dough, no go," and then sarcastically observed that if I did not run for financial reasons, my example might change the course of American politics. Why? Because everyone felt that the "ego food" of the bright lights would always blind one's common sense!

Traveling across the country, I found that men and women, from college students to senior citizens, wanted politicians who understand what is going on in their lives and government policies that reflect that understanding. Audiences asked questions about my personal life, to make sure I wasn't just spouting rhetoric. "How do you work and have a family?" and "What did you do about child care?" were questions that made it clear Americans were desperate for someone to help them juggle all the roles and chores modern life has laid upon them. One August day, I gave a keynote speech on family issues twice in Portland, Oregon, first to the National Women's Political Caucus and then to the National Association of Postmasters of America. With the first audience, I was preaching to the converted, but I didn't know what to expect from the postmasters. The average age of the crowd was about fifty, and the placards of the various delegations indicated that there was a heavy concentration from the southern states. The meeting began with the Lord's Prayer. As I talked about the need for parents to have time off with their babies, I could see heads nodding in agreement. I

discussed "empty nests" and the "comeback kids," my name
for the new generation of young people who may be better
educated than their parents but cannot find jobs that pay well
enough for them to move out of their parents' homes. Heads
kept nodding. When I finished, there was a standing ovation,
proof to me that my message about getting the government
to help families was one that transcended geographic, gener-
ational, gender and socioeconomic differences.

It became clear that people want the American family to
thrive and are deeply worried about it. I continue to be dismayed that most other countries in the developed world do
much more to help families than we do, with far better statistics on divorce, infant mortality and adolescent problems.
I think there's a connection. Politicians have viewed family
issues as good buzzwords in speeches but not worth addressing in policy. Colleagues tell me legislative family issues are
too vague a concept to mobilize a constituency around. Liberals say that the right wing has stolen family issues, and we
can't reclaim them. They're wrong. The right has stolen the
talk, but scatter rapidly when you try and act.

Citizens understood how the federal government left
families to fend for themselves, while spending the treasury
into the red in order to serve as the world's military 911
number. Americans are generous and have always rallied to
play their role on the world scene. In postwar times, our
Japanese and European allies had booming economies,
with paid health care, free college tuition and excellent

child care for their citizens. They could afford these programs because we denied them to ourselves in order to provide the world's military defense. The United States continues to act as if World War II had just ended. When I was in the House, I argued it was time for a little burden sharing by our allies. Many politicians called me an isolationist and treated me like a skunk at a garden party. But my support was seen in the volunteers who sponsored "Run, Pat, Run" fund-raisers all over the country. I made a video for each of them to show, explaining why I wanted to be a candidate and what I meant when I said it was time America have a "Rendezvous with Reality." Our allies had prospered since the war and now could do their fair share. That was the only way we could deal with our debt and family issues.

One of my moments of truth on the 1987 campaign trail was when I was introduced in a southern state by the Democratic state chairman. He was saying glowing things: that he admired my style, that he'd love to have a woman in the White House, that I knew more about national defense than all of the other candidates combined. I felt like I'd been sitting on a helium air hose—I was all puffed up. Then the bubble burst. "Of course I can't vote for her," he said, "because I have a problem with a man for First Lady." What do you say as you step to the mike after that line?

I was both amused and annoyed by some of the questions that came up. "Does your husband know you're running?" (Yes, I'd mentioned it.) Or "How do you wear your hair when you're dressed up?" (I really favor an orange mohawk—this salt-and-pepper pageboy is just a political cover.) "Why are you running as a woman?" (Like, what are my other choices?)

By August I was third in the *Time* magazine poll—very exciting, but third doesn't cut it. The National Organization for Women had pledged about $400,000, enough to qualify me for federal matching funds in several states. Some women's groups withheld their support, concerned about the symbolism of another woman losing a national election so soon after Geraldine Ferraro's unsuccessful bid to be vice president. (Gary Hart conspicuously endorsed Mario Cuomo, who was not even running.) But I didn't have enough money to be truly competitive. All along, people had been saying, "It would be really interesting if you ran," and I thought that meant they would support me. Some did, and some just thought: *How nice—the race is more interesting.* It was a reality check: I wanted to be president, not interesting! Other politicians were hesitant to put their own careers on the line by actively saying I was a viable candidate. Victoria Woodhull in 1872, Belva Lockwood in 1884, Shirley Chisholm in 1972 and Pat Schroeder in 1987 all found that the White House is still America's ultimate clubhouse with a "No Girls Allowed" sign posted.

Jim tried to talk me out of quitting the race, but my pragmatism prevailed. Walking onto the stage to address hundreds of supporters on a beautiful September day in

Denver, I knew the speech was going to be tricky. My message was a paradox: My summer exploration had been so successful that I was not going to run. I wanted to make clear that my decision was based on my knowledge that winning would take a lot more preparation, time and money than I had. As I took a deep breath and approached the microphone, I could see my parents, who had never known me to back down before. My father was so sure I would go the distance that when a California vendor who had been supplying us with campaign buttons called to ask about rumors that I was not going to run, Dad laughed and said that was just a ploy to keep the press guessing. She made more buttons, so for years I had favors for interns, auctions and other events.

When I reached the crucial part of my speech and said I would not be running for president, the crowd groaned. People shouted, "No, no," and began to chant "Run, Pat, run." My heart sank, and I began to cry. I had underestimated how much I wanted to pursue the presidency. I went on with my speech, but it was my tears, not my words, that got the headlines. Those seventeen seconds were treated like a total breakdown.

For weeks afterward, there were columns pro and con on my reaction. Some writers went so far as to say that my tears had dampened all hopes for women in presidential politics for the rest of this century. "She's the stereotype of women as weepy wimps who don't belong in the business of serious affairs," raged a New York columnist. "What a devastating indictment of this girl's character," screamed another. (Excuse me, *girl?*) A writer for the *Washington Post* wrote, "I'm starting to feel pretty cynical about the kinds of examples our most famous elder sisters are setting for us young women." Meg Greenfield, the op-ed page editor of the *Post*, invited me to give my perspective. I recalled that Kennedy aide Ted Sorenson had once introduced me as a politician who can "draft a bill, stir a crowd, fly a plane, bake a cake, pass a law, coin a phrase—and run for president." When I got up to the podium, I corrected him on one count: "I know a bakery that delivers." But in the article I added one other item to his list: "And wears her heart on her sleeve." The critics who infuriated me the most were those who said they wouldn't want the person who had a "finger on the nuclear button" to be someone who cries. I wouldn't want that person to be someone who *doesn't* cry!

I decided I could make a fortune marketing Schroeder teardrop jewelry or endorsing Kleenex. But at least crying came out of the closet. Joseph Califano told me that during his farewell speech, after Jimmy Carter fired him as secretary of health, education and welfare, he cried uncontrollably. A constituent wrote and reminded me that President Lyndon Johnson sobbed through a civil rights ceremony at the White House. A lobbyist sent me the story of George Washington's farewell dinner with his revolutionary war generals, when there was hugging and crying all around the table. I started my "sob sister" file. What do

Mikhail Gorbachev, Norman Schwarzkopf, Ronald Reagan, Margaret Thatcher, Chile's General Pinochet, John Sununu, Illinois Governor Jim Thompson, Oliver North, George Bush, minority leader Bob Michael, California Speaker Willie Brown, almost every famous American athlete and Pat Schroeder have in common? We're sob sisters. We're all in the weep-stakes. Now crying is almost a ritual that male politicians must do to prove they are compassionate, but women are supposed to wear iron britches.

There was a satisfying footnote to the crying incident. Awhile later I took the family to San Diego to see the Denver Broncos play the Washington Redskins in the Super Bowl. The four of us had to share one big room at the Del Coronado Hotel. Reservations were tight and we were late in deciding to go. The Broncos played miserably. We wanted to shed our team-spirited orange clothes and sneak out of the stadium but felt an indecent exposure arrest would not be a great boost to my career.

After dinner, accompanied by a lot of razzing from the Redskins fans, we went back to the hotel for the great family slumber party. The kids turned on the TV and were suddenly howling and rolling on the floor. This was a phenomenal mood change, and I hurried out of the bathroom to discover what had triggered it. There I was, or at least a reasonable facsimile of me: salt-and-pepper hair, big teeth, aqua suit and a box of Kleenex. Nora Dunn was doing Pat Schroeder on *Saturday Night Live*.

Several years later I received an invitation to address a Washington press group, which is one of the worst tribal rites in town. There is a mandate to be funny, but people sit there with their arms folded on their chests. They look like they were weaned on pickles and dare the speaker to elicit laughs. I called Nora Dunn to ask if she would come impersonate me, and she said yes. The plan was for me to sit at the head table for dinner, then excuse myself before dessert and go to the restroom. Nora would come back, wearing the identical dress, and take my place at the table. Then she would approach the microphone to do my gig, and I'd run in from the back of the room saying, "Who is that woman?"

Nora was certain she would be discovered when she replaced me at the head table. I was sitting between two colleagues in the House Democratic leadership, men I worked with every day. "I'll be busted," she kept saying, despite my assurances that most politicians barely registered another person's presence, especially if the other person was female. I was right. When Nora sat down at my table and started eating the dessert, no one even noticed. When she went to the microphone, I ran up the aisle, unmasking her as an impostor. The audience howled. But the joke had a sad subtext: It was so easy for two women to pull off this prank. Like "Mr. Cellophane" in the show *Chicago,* no one ever knows we're there. Or maybe they know it but just want to ignore it.

8

Domestic Engineering

It's been thrilling to be on the front lines of culture-cracking and to shepherd historic changes for women, yet I wonder what the family culture will be like in the twenty-first century. I hope it won't be Martha Stewartville, with those perfectly posed family pictures, neatly framed in her well-ordered home. The chaotic, messy contingencies of family life don't make great photo ops. I hope our new culture will realize the hypocrisy of a home that beautifully showcases a family but never shelters one.

During my years in Congress, I heard every bad joke about marriage imaginable ("I didn't know what happiness was until I was married, and then it was too late") from the same colleagues who preach about family values every time they get near a microphone. Praising marriage and family in public, but privately refusing to invest the time required to make it a success, seems to me the height of cynicism and hypocrisy. One colleague had a bumper sticker on his car that he parked in the House garage that read, "Wife and dog missing. Reward for dog."

My childhood home was never the island of tranquillity romanticized in my high school home ec books—we were too nomadic for that—and neither was my children's childhood home. They had to assume early responsibility for domestic duties that their less-than-perfect mother could not fit into the day. I find it amazing that kids can use almost all new technology much better than their parents but are challenged by dishwashers, washing machines and dryers. If our kids grumbled about doing their own laundry, I had a lowly trick: I'd ruin one of their favorite items with a little bleach in the wash. When Scott went to college, he brought his friends home for laundry instruction. He was proud of his survival skills.

In 1973 career women were a rare breed. I felt I was performing a heroic act every day I got through. It was always tempting to use public opportunities to portray myself as the perfect chef, housekeeper, gardener. The truth is, I am fairly hopeless at traditional domesticity. The kids said we never had to worry about holes in our window screens because my food didn't even attract flies. Jim joked that I must have thought he was a god because I put so many burnt offerings in front of him. The family never stops teasing about my "chainsaw" brownies. (I forget to take them out of the oven, rendering them impossible to cut with an ordinary knife.) So rather than deal in fantasy, I prepared a "recipe" to send whenever one was requested by a women's group or magazine:

A Schroeder Breakfast: Find a bowl. If it's on the floor, wash it because the dog has probably used it. Find some cereal. Hopefully, it will be sugar-coated so you don't have to go on a scavenger hunt for the sugar. Then get milk from the refrigerator. But it is imperative that you read the spoil date before using. When these items have been located, assemble.

My recipes were rarely included in anthologies, and I often got letters saying my staff was sabotaging me. Look what they sent out! Because I was cooking-impaired, I always avoided one of the tribal rites taken so seriously by members of Congress, the annual chili cook-off. But one year, Garaldine Price, wife of Mel Price, the chairman of the Armed Services Committee, called and begged me to participate. "Just do it your way," she said. So I found a recipe in the *Colorado Junior League Cookbook* and got a caterer to make it. If someone had asked, I wouldn't have been able to identify my own bowl of chili since I'd never seen it. I won first prize. Mrs. Price was frantic. "Don't tell a soul what you did," she said. "The others spent all weekend cooking." I felt awful holding the trophy for photos.

Shortly before I left Congress, my office got a request from a new cable channel devoted to gardening that wanted to showcase my yard. My staff explained that the Schroeders really didn't have a garden, but the producer was insistent. "Oh, everyone says that," she countered. "I'm sure Mrs. Schroeder would love to show us around." My neighbor, who has lovely manicured flower beds, offered to exchange houses, but in the interest of full disclosure, I let the gardening-show people come over on a Sunday morning to take snapshots. They never clicked the camera as I showed them my hanging baskets and beds of silk flowers, explaining how they bloomed even in the dead of winter. They were horrified, and I was not on the show.

It is hopeful that as women move into new skill areas that the gender known for being helpmates is beginning to translate this skill into help for the political sisterhood. A study from Rutgers University's Center for the American Woman and Politics found that women in the state legislature were more apt to help other women rather than male colleagues. This is great news. The study also found that women favored government in the public view over closed-door politics and wanted elected officials to be more responsive to groups denied full access to the policy-making process. But in my early congressional experience, the community support received by other minority representatives was much stronger than the support I got in the women's community. When Hispanic, Asian or African-American legislators pushed bills benefiting or boosting their community, there were cheers. From the beginning I always had a long list of bills benefiting women, children and families—all the new legislative ground I wanted to plow. I was sure my female colleagues would be eager to join in the advocacy. How surprised I was when they often argued that I was moving too fast and pushing too hard. I had a recurrent dream that I was pushing a wheelbarrow loaded with my bills up a mountain, with rubber handles so it kept rolling back on me!

Perhaps other women feared that if I did not fully succeed and shine, they personally would be labeled as failures. There seemed to be a notion that women were like bowling pins: If one got knocked down, we all could go. The solution was to put great distance between each other and hope we would survive on our own. I'm always disappointed by the lack of courage or probity or vision in women. Even more discouraging is how hard we have to fight for the smallest gains. Let me tell you a story about a marble statue.

In 1893 the Columbia World Exposition in Chicago was organized to celebrate the four-hundredth anniversary of Christopher Columbus discovering the New World. Women on the organizing board felt that since Queen Isabella put up the money for the *Niña*, the *Pinta* and the *Santa Maria*, there should be an area of the exposition honoring women. That opinion got the women thrown off the board. One of them was a socialite named Bertha Palmer, who was married to the owner of Chicago's Palmer House Hotel. She and others purchased land adjacent to the fair and put together their own exhibit. The Women's International Congress was governed by a 117-member Board of Lady Managers who worked to display women's contributions to world culture. They even provided full-service day care. The women's exhibit was so popular that twenty-seven million people visited in the six months it was open. It was the only part of the Exposition that did not run a deficit. A sculptor named Adelaide Johnson was hired to create a statue of three courageous suffragettes: Elizabeth Cady Stanton, Susan B. Anthony and Lucretia Mott.

When women won the vote in 1920, none of these suffragettes were alive, but money was collected from all over the country for a statue to honor them in Washington. Adelaide Johnson was selected as the sculptor. She enhanced the statue she did for the fair. The sculpture was carved out of eight tons of white marble, showing the women from the waist up. It was a metaphor for their emergence from the subjugation of society. On Susan B. Anthony's birthday, February 15, 1921, congressional leaders accepted the statue in the Capitol rotunda as a gift from the American people, celebrating our foremothers' leadership and courage. Several days later, after some strong drinks, senior congressional leaders decided to send the statue to the basement. Elizabeth Cady Stanton, Susan B. Anthony and Lucretia Mott just weren't cute enough for the old bulls, then or now: Even recently I heard some of my own colleagues call the sculpture "three ugly women in a bathtub." In 1995 Senator John Warner (Republican from Virginia) introduced a bill to bring the statue back to the Rotunda, and it was unanimously passed. It was hard to imagine that anyone in the House would object, but a freshman woman from North Carolina, one of Newt Gingrich's acolytes, protested, saying it was unfair to use $75,000 in taxpayers' money to move the statue. (Where was she when taxpayers funded the placing of male statues in the Capitol?) A group of private businesswomen raised the money to move the suffragettes, but it still required congressional approval. Finally, in 1997, after a long battle, the statue was returned to its original place.

This episode saddened me because it speaks to women's self-esteem. No congressman would ever say a statue of a male leader was not a big enough deal to have the public pay for its placement in the Capitol. These three women were responsible for more than half of American citizens gaining the right to vote and yet were not deemed worthy enough for public funding of their being elevated from the basement. The fact that this was the doing of a female congressional colleague is pretty depressing.

But while I sound like I'm whining, I admit that from the beginning some of my strongest support came from a dynamic sisterhood. The Women's Leadership Project, headed by Laura A. Liswood, produced a brilliant film consisting of interviews with current and former female heads of state. All of them were asked exactly the same questions about their achievements, tribulations and concerns. It is stunning how similar the women's answers were, even though the women and their cultures were starkly different. The comment I liked the best was that no woman would even think of organizing a government without men in it, but men do it all the time without women. Liswood said that when the cameras were turned off, her interviewees would often ask what the other heads of state had said. Obviously, they too felt like pioneers, very much alone and curious about how other pioneers were doing.

Professionally, we women are afraid to express anything less than perfect professional contentment for fear of hearing, "If you can't take it, give your job back to the man you shouldn't have supplanted in the first place." We bottle up our feelings, afraid of being labeled whiners. When women in the military were subjected to harassment and worse, the political writer George Will suggested that they should be removed from the service. Obviously it was clear to him the women were the problem.

His attitude was not surprising, since Will was one of

my early debating opponents on ERA. Toward the end of my career, he was still attacking me vigorously. This time it was because I was promoting "midnight basketball": Inner-city kids who did their homework in study halls got to play basketball at night as a reward. The result was that kids were actually staying in school and learning. Selfless volunteers had to organize the program, find the kids, find the space, raise money to pay the janitors and insurance costs for keeping the schools open at night, and then work on their own time for the study halls and the games. With a small contribution from the government, we could free these good folks up to spend time with the kids instead of running around soliciting corporate donors. Will thought the program was fine if the private sector paid for it, but he didn't want any federal money going to the program. I still can't think of a better use for tax dollars.

There is a lot of progress. Federal enforcement of Title IX has given young women a menu of choices in school. But there is no Title IX equivalent in the workplace, and when women enter the job market often they suddenly discover discrimination is still alive and well. Many of them roared into my office while I was in Congress to complain about the unfairness of lower pay or favoritism shown to men. I'd say, "Welcome to feminism." They'd insist they were not feminists. I don't know how we lost these young women or how they came to associate feminism with mythical acts like bra-burning. It's also discouraging to see we only get them back when they personally hit the discrimination wall. It becomes real only when it happens to them.

Even the best-intentioned people remain woefully ignorant about the serious harm to women justified by tradition. The practice of female genital mutilation (FGM) in certain parts of the world speaks volumes about the global status of women. I didn't learn about it until I was in Congress. President Sadat had appointed the first woman to head the Egyptian Public Health Service. When she wrote a book about FGM and how many young girls die from it in Egypt each year, she ended up in prison. When I was in Egypt for the 1994 United Nations International Conference on Population and Development, I decided to do everything I could to attack this practice. There was tremendous discussion about the barbaric tradition of clitoral mutilation, sometimes performed in the home with a paring knife. This act has no basis in health or religion. (There is no mention of the practice in the Koran, and the head of the Coptic Christian Church in Egypt stated publicly that there was no reason for it.) It is estimated that more than 100 million girls and women around the world have undergone this brutal procedure, leading to devastating harm, pain, virtual elimination of sexual pleasure and sometimes death. The head of a hospital in Cairo, where international groups were holding a seminar on why this should be outlawed, said, "You're talking bunk here." Meanwhile, another man came in and bragged, "My daughter is having this procedure done right now." He invited those of us at the hospital to his home. I choked, but the camera crew from CNN went and filmed the little girl screaming as a barber cut her clitoris.

When that film aired, engendering global outrage, Egyptian Minister of Health Ali Abdel Fattah stated that FGM should be banned and those who perform it punished. A month later, apparently under political pressure, he issued a directive permitting public hospitals to perform FGM. In 1995, again after international protest about his "medicalizing" the procedure, this directive was rescinded, and a new directive stated that medical personnel would be limited to counseling about the practice. In 1996, the new health minister, Ismail Sallam, extended the ban to cover private hospitals as well, prohibiting any licensed medical professional from performing FGM. In 1997, an Egyptian court overturned the ban. The presiding judge declared, "Doctors' right to perform their profession according to the law—which allows them to do surgery—cannot be restricted by a ministerial decree." The sheikh who was suing the minister of health over this issue claimed he would strive to have expurgated from schoolbooks any mention of the negative impact of female circumcision and have it replaced with the "correct" teaching that such a practice is a must. Just four days prior to the court's decision, an eleven-year-old girl had died as a result of this procedure, performed by a doctor.

International groups are so much more reticent to push for women's rights than human rights. Are we not human?

Those who take an "America first" approach to solving social problems know that FGM is not limited to Egypt. It goes on in countless ethnic communities in this country, surreptitiously and silently, with the same predictably appalling results. It is known by other sanitized names, but I think it is child abuse and am proud I finally got my legislation passed making it illegal in this country.

Despite some well-orchestrated attempts to present a more judicious public image, one of the worst bastions of discrimination against women in our own country is still in the military. For two dozen years my office was the ombudsman for female members of the armed forces who were made to feel they were persona non grata in their place of work. The military never invited women in. When President Truman desegregated the armed services, they were forced to deal with African Americans as equals, yet even then equality was a long time coming.

Women never had a Trumanesque command from on high. The conventional wisdom in the military is that women were forced on them for social experimentation. No high-level person wants to challenge this conventional wisdom by saying, "You're all part of the team, so treat each other with the respect teammates deserve." To challenge this thinking would make them unpopular with the uniformed leaders. So year after year American women have been second-class citizens in the U.S. military and no one seems to care.

The recent rash of headline-making stories about sexual misconduct in the services was no surprise to me. I heard stories just like these all through my years in Congress. I believe the only reason such stories are finally deemed newsworthy is that the Cold War is over. During a time of high military preparedness, such conduct was minimized because there was too much other *important* business to cover. The annual Tailhook convention didn't *just* get out of hand recently—it had been an escalating contest of bad behavior for years, where men engaged in capturing women and shaving their legs in the lobbies of their hotels, running women through paddle lines, destroying property and hiring call girls. They often made some highly unflattering T-shirts and performed skits about me. But Tailhook misbehavior was always a one-day story. The press would exonerate the behavior with a wink and then acknowledge that our fighting men deserved to blow off some steam. Then it was back to focusing on the Russians.

Over the years I watched as female military careers were blocked, sometimes with subtle measures. The flight schools were opened to women, but not the billets the schools prepared them for. One day a certain billet would be open to them, and the next day it would be closed.

They'd been tested more than any other group in the military and always received the highest marks, but certain doors remained firmly shut. There were women who finished first in their flight training, which cost approximately a quarter of a million dollars, and they were allowed only to teach combat missions, not fly them. Clearly the airmen in the position of being trained by someone who had never done what she taught harbored great resentment. It is such a stupid waste of resources.

When I went to the Air Force Academy to talk to students, both male and female, the young men started railing about women's "special privileges." What special privileges?

"Well, they get to wear earrings," I was told.

"Okay," I reasoned, "does it affect the mission?"

"No, it doesn't," they said.

"Do you want to wear earrings?" I asked.

"Hell, no," they said. Then they complained that "women get to wear their hair long."

"Does it affect the mission?" I asked.

"No," they said.

"Do *you* want to have long hair?"

"Hell, no," they said. This went on and on, with young women sitting next to them. A way to crack these attitudes must be found.

In the late seventies I was visiting the Lowry Air Force Base in Denver and a group of female officers approached me. They told me that they were supposed to use the Officers' Club, but the topless dancers performing there made it quite uncomfortable for them. I called Dr. Sheila E. Widnall, then undersecretary of the Air Force and now secretary, who was appalled—topless dancing in an officers' club was strictly against regulations. She immediately sent out an order. I thought I was so smart and felt good that I'd solved the problem. *Wrong.* A few months later, I heard from the women at Lowry that nothing had changed. I asked for an investigation. It turned out that the uniformed men in the secretary's office had never bothered to send out her order; they thought she was just making noise and didn't really intend any action to be taken.

Another reason so little progress has been made is that feminist groups have never fully supported women in the armed forces. Many of them came from the peace movement and were very conflicted about military service by anyone—male or female. Some of the most painful fights I ever had were with good friends who couldn't understand my concerns and efforts for women in the military. "But *we* don't want to be in the army," they'd say. There seemed to be a concern that women in the military were NOK—Not Our Kind. Meanwhile, many males argued they were all lesbians and pregnant. I pointed out that was usually an oxymoron—rather like military intelligence.

9

Take the Eye of a Newt . . .

The office of the Speaker of the House looks like the lobby of a medium-size hotel: lots of chairs to accommodate a steady stream of visitors. Usually each Speaker brings in some furnishings from his home state to try to make the office look a little more like Oklahoma or Massachusetts or Texas. (Newt Gingrich got a dinosaur. I don't think it is from Georgia, so I'm not sure what the message is.)

It is not axiomatic that the most charismatic person in the House becomes Speaker. The decision of who is elected Speaker has more to do with the image the party in power wants to project than anything else. If there's one trait all Speakers share, it's that they've survived some tough political contests: The route to the Speaker's chair can be long and bloody. In general, the parties elect their whip, who almost automatically becomes majority leader when his party's in power, and then almost automatically Speaker.

When I arrived in Congress, I was sworn in by Carl Albert, an honorable man from Bugtussle, Oklahoma. Micro-mini in size, Albert gave Senator Barbara Mikulski a great story. When she first came to Congress, a proud young Polish-American woman representing a district in Baltimore, she was invited to address the press corps at an elegant dinner. She carefully shopped for her outfit, only to be demolished when she entered the hotel that evening and heard someone say, "Hey, look, it's Carl Albert in drag." The barons liked Albert because they thought they could push around such a mild-mannered man. His own party was sure he would not embarrass or bulldoze or deny—he was kind of a place holder. He was Speaker during Watergate, which was not the easiest time to be Speaker—he was even in line to be president after Spiro Agnew resigned and before Nixon appointed Ford. The end of Albert's career in Congress was tainted by "Korea-gate," when Korean businessmen were accused of trying to peddle influence with American government officials, and in 1976 he stepped down.

Tip O'Neill left a more lasting legacy by the force of his personality. I rarely needed a formal appointment to see him because he was the most reachable Speaker by far. He was always schlepping through the cloakroom, stopping to chat and smoking a cigar. He hated TV appearances and press conferences. He had the classic "radio face," and some in our party complained he wasn't telegenic enough.

But he and Ronald Reagan were perfectly matched: two Irishmen who loved to tell stories. (One of my favorite Tip stories had to do with his taking Sargent Shriver into the bars of South Boston to commune with "the common man" during Sarge's 1972 run for vice president. Tip told Shriver: "All you have to do is say, 'The drinks are on me,' and you'll have it made." They went in to a bar, Tip introduced him as "the next vice president of the United States" and Shriver delivered the right line. But when the bartender asked him what he was drinking, Shriver replied, "Courvoisier with a twist.")

The Republicans saw that Tip was a great counterweight to the Reagan charm and began attacking him in ads. They had a lookalike actor driving a car that was running out of gas, supposedly symbolic of Democratic programs. They tried to paint him as an old-time machine pol whose ideas had lost their impetus. But people *liked* Tip, and nothing the Republican spin doctors did could tarnish that reputation. Even *Reagan* liked him. The two men would meet on an issue they vehemently disagreed about—one for killing Social Security, one for expanding it—spend the meeting swapping stories and being conciliatory, and then say to their respective staffs, "You guys make it all work"—an impossible task for the idealogues on both staffs.

Jim Wright, who succeeded Tip in 1987, was more in the LBJ mold, gleeful and overt in using the knobs of control. He was a sharp partisan player who saw himself as a power broker. He didn't hang out in the cloakroom, preferring to address an audience. He could give a hell of a speech. He was a hell of a vote counter, too: He knew down to every last man and woman how a vote would come in. But Wright had written a book and he had figured out a way to use it to circumvent the rules about profiting from speeches. There were limits to what a congressman could collect for giving a speech, but Wright would give a speech and get the speech's sponsors to buy a few hundred copies of his book. His royalty payments on the book added a sweetener. Hardly defensible, but pretty penny-ante stuff compared with Newt Gingrich trying to cut a multi-million-dollar book deal with Rupert Murdoch's publishing company.

Wright lost his speakership over his flaunting of the rules. Newt had to return most of the money, but never admitted his book deal was a convenient way to channel money into his back pocket. When he went on tour to publicize his book, his promotional appearances were more like political rallies.

The morale of House Democrats was in the toilet when Tom Foley became Speaker in 1989. He was a gentleman and a scholar—many Democrats worried that he wouldn't be partisan enough. I thought he would have made a great judge, since he was always trying to be fair and balanced. As party whip, when he was supposed to be rounding up votes for the Democratic bills, he'd come talk to me and explain why some people might vote yes on a particular measure, and then I'd find out the party vote was no! Fairness is great, but when you have terrorists at the door, fairness loses. It was Foley's responsibility to appoint the committee members that heard Oliver North's testimony during the Iran-Contra hearings. Chairman Lee Hamilton (Democrat from Indiana) was measured, considerate, thoughtful, bright—and he had his head bitten off by North and Brendan Sullivan, North's pit-bull lawyer, who was worth every penny he was paid. (I also thought that whoever did Ollie's puppy-dog eyes for the hearing was not paid enough.) To have that hearing take place in a Democratic-controlled House was unimaginable. We came in every day with barf bags.

When the House check-writing scandal broke out, Foley did not understand how serious it was: Many congressmen and -women had been writing checks over and above their accounts in the House bank. I never knew I could write "bad" checks and had never taken advantage of those services. When the news broke and it was revealed that I had written four bad checks, I took all of my banking records to the local papers in Denver and I decided to get to the bottom of this.

We never even saw our paychecks in Congress. Once a month, they were given directly to the sergeant at arms, with deductions made for FICA and Social Security, and then deposited into our House accounts. But the "bankers" were political appointees, not people with financial experience. If the person assigned to oversee my account wasn't around when checks came in to be deposited, the checks were just stuck in a drawer, sometimes for weeks.

I gave a lot of speeches, but under House rules I was not allowed to accept payment. So the organization I spoke to would pay me, and I'd write a check for that amount in the name of some charity. The four "hot" checks were all ones that I had written to charities.

In the end, the scandal was a case of sloppy bookkeeping—no real bank could keep its books that way. Foley kept downplaying the severity of the scandal, insisting, "It's not really a bank." But to people in Dubuque, Iowa, or Mobile, Alabama, it was a bank, and they didn't let us forget it in the next election. Our leaders kept saying, "We've been more efficient than any other Congress! We got the budget out on time!" But it didn't matter. The perception was that we were crooks, trying to lob one over on the American public.

Part of the problem was that Foley's wife was his chief of staff. With most chiefs of staff, you can be honest, even blunt. But who's going to say, "Has he lost his *mind*?" to the wife of the Speaker?

Foley's career sadly unraveled over the Brady Bill. His home state of Washington has a strong National Rifle Association membership, and Foley had always voted *against* gun control of any kind. When the Brady Bill passed out of committee, the NRA felt Foley should have used his position as Speaker to block it, so it would not come to the floor for a full House vote. But Foley didn't use his power that way. He was fair. The NRA started an all-out campaign against him, and he lost his seat in 1994. That was the year the Republicans swept into office, so Foley would not have been Speaker even if he had been reelected.

After his defeat, I read an amazing story that a high percentage of voters in his district thought the guy who beat him, George Nethercutt, would be the new Speaker. I guess they thought the fifth district of Washington owned the Speaker's chair! But as every House Democrat knew immediately, the next Speaker of the House would be Newt Gingrich.

———————————

The ascension of Newt Gingrich to the position of Speaker meant that I had no legislative responsibility at all. He cared not a whit what bills I wanted to pass. There was no communication from the Speaker's office to the Democratic caucus—we were actually passing notes around to find out things like: What time are we going to start tomorrow? I don't think that the Democratic leader, Dick Gephardt, was ever invited to Gingrich's office. The

Republicans were on such a high, they were having nose-bleeds. There was no support from the Democratic Party. Our members had not yet learned to work together, each thinking they'd all cut their own deals with the new guy. Even the moderate Republicans were playing "get along, go along"—fearful that they could lose their positions in the House. They didn't fear Gingrich as much as the power of the new hard-liners in Congress that were elected in 1994.

But in a strange way, Newt provided some of the most fun I had in politics. I couldn't wait to get the newspapers every day and see what he'd said or done in the last twenty-four hours. Every now and then he'd be silenced by horri-fied Republican officials. Yet he could never go more than a few days without a media fix. He'd break out of the duct tape to make another one of his phenomenal faux pas. I feared that eventually his party would find a muzzle he couldn't break, and my life would return to routine legisla-tive rhythms. But my fear never materialized. Newt could not seem to learn to engage his brain before starting his mouth. He gave me much more material than I ever had time to work with. I loved it.

Newt had managed to get some conservative founda-tions to bankroll him in preparing a course for a small col-lege in Georgia, but it was less of a political science lec-ture and more of a right-wing diatribe. Since his talks were aired on cable TV, there were all sorts of questionable issues under the House ethics laws about whether it was legal for him to have this format to air his agenda (especially since all of the legislation deregulating cable was in front of Congress that year). But the ethics code of the House might as well have been written in pig Latin. No group is good at policing its own. And no member wants to serve on the ethics committee: Everything is done in closed session. Members get no political benefit in their home district for their efforts. Charges were filed against Newt, some of which were dismissed for technical reasons, but on the rest no action was taken until the beginning of the next session. He quickly pleaded guilty to some of the charges and borrowed $300,000 from Bob Dole to help pay his fine.

It was during one of his infamous college lectures that he said men were better in war because they were like piglets, prone to rolling around in the trenches and born with a primal urge to hunt giraffes. Life in the trenches would be more difficult for women, he said, because they got infections. I was fascinated with his theories and got a transcript. I thought such wisdom should be shared with other members of Congress. I took the House floor and read the lecture—great theater that was picked up on lots of news broadcasts. When I returned to Denver that weekend, an old friend brought me a beautifully framed pill from "Newt Laboratories," which has had a place of honor on my wall ever since. The inscription reads:

The laboratories of the National Empowerment for Women Today (NEWT) are pleased to announce the development of their new product: Anti-feminine trench infection pill.

WARNING!

Possible side effects:

1. Sudden urges to roll around in trenches, as piglets are wont to do.

2. Unexpected desire to cross traditional gender limits and embark upon primitive giraffe-hunting expeditions.

3. Inability to sit calmly before radar and/or television screens for extended periods of time.

4. Compulsive need to seek out $4,500,000.00 book deals. At NEWT Labs our motto is:

"We protect the woman you love."

Newt handed me another great opportunity to score political points the day he stomped off *Air Force One* because the president didn't stroke his ego properly. Newspaper headlines called him "crybaby." I had a fake Oscar in my closet. (My staff used to tease me that I had more props than a Vegas showgirl. I'd used them for child-rearing incentives, like Best Performance for an Increase in Allowance, and I never throw anything away.) At the beginning of each day of Congress, members are permitted one-minute speeches (whoever is controlling the House that day decides how many members will get to speak on each side). It's a venting session, and it's relayed on C-SPAN, so it gets good play. I got to do one of the one-minute rants for the Democratic side. I pulled out the Oscar to nominate Newt Gingrich for the Best Performance by a Child Actor this year. I didn't feel at all guilty. Newt used to specialize in that kind of attack himself, especially when we got cameras in the House. This little gambit came right out of his legislative terrorism manual!

I enjoyed punching back, but it was not all in jest. Many days I felt like a Pekingese yapping at a pit bull. Actually, I was aware of Newt even before his first victory, when he was running against a state senator in Georgia named Virginia Shepherd. Georgia had elected no women to Congress. Shepherd had a reputation for being savvy, classy and able to get things done in a political body that did not welcome her. I went to stump for her because the idea of electing such a terrific woman to Congress would be a huge boost. In the South, political women had trouble breaking through. Newt started vicious attacks against her, charging that she was a lousy wife and mother who was running for office to escape her family. ("What kind of woman would leave her husband and children . . . ?") Later the world was to learn that these allegations were really revelations about Newt's own life, a syndrome that psychoanalysts call "projecting": He was divorcing his first wife, who was ill with breast cancer. I found that Newt continued this pattern of projection throughout his congressional career. If he accused someone of a certain behavior, it usually meant he was doing it himself. It was amazing that he could have gotten away with making Virginia Shepherd "antifamily," but his allegations stuck, and she lost the election.

Whenever Congress doesn't have enough guts to deal with something directly, it finds "independent authorities" and says: We'll have to do what they recommend. In 1990 a "blue-ribbon panel" of businessmen in the private sector was commissioned to determine how much of a salary raise congressmen were entitled to receive. Surprise, surprise: The recommendation was for a huge increase. (Can you imagine such a group that makes its living by asking for congressional favors saying, "After careful study, we've decided the pay scale is about right"?) The Democratic leadership of Congress (Speaker Tom Foley, majority leader Dick Gephardt and the committee chairs) agreed not to work against Gingrich in his campaign for reelection because he supported the congressional pay raise. I was stunned and disobeyed orders from on high when I helped Dave Worley, the energetic, red-haired Georgia lawyer who was running against Gingrich. Newt won by a few hundred votes—officially it was a fifty-fifty race. I'll always be sorry that I didn't publicly expose the stupidity of the Democratic leadership for protecting him, foolishly believing that they could exact some sort of quid pro quo.

Gingrich emasculated the Congressional Caucus on

Women's Issues. According to House rules, we could divert money that was earmarked for our individual staffs to the caucus, pool it and hire people just to work on women's issues. Gingrich took away that ability. He also took away the right of the caucus to have an office on the Hill. Suddenly we had to pay caucus staffers and rent with money raised from special interests and sympathetic supporters. Obviously it was also more cumbersome to keep in touch with the members. The caucus is still limping along under those thwarted conditions.

The only thing that brought Newt and me together was dragons. Indonesia has beautiful Komodo dragons that look like something out of a fairy tale, and the ones living at the Washington Zoo had just had babies. I wanted to get them for the Denver Zoo, and Newt wanted them for the Atlanta Zoo. I'm sure that in the eyes of many, this unnatural team was thought of as the Dragon Lady and the Dragon Lord. Luckily there were enough dragons to satisfy both of our constituencies, without a partisan struggle.

In my last congressional term, Gingrich and I had a final face-off when he bullied the Department of Defense into "lending" him about $250,000 worth of D.O.D. staff for his office. I was impudent enough to ask publicly who were those military officers in his office, and was this legal? After an investigation by the Government Accounting Office decided the placement was illegal and the officers were being used for political purposes, Newt's wrath toward me was fanned. I wasn't scared of him—what did he have that I wanted? But it soon became clear just how strong a political enemy he was.

I was preparing to go to Stockholm for the Organization for Security and Cooperation in Europe (OSCE), the parliamentary assembly for legislative members of countries who signed the Helsinki Accords. Heads of state meet all the time but not parliaments, and the OSCE was like a living laboratory for government. During the Cold War, the OSCE monitored human rights behind the Iron Curtain. It was a phenomenal tool to support indigent groups. It continued to work in the former Yugoslavia, Albania, Turkey and other emerging democracies. It's easy to talk the talk about freedom, not so easy to help them walk the walk. The day before the congressional delegation was to leave, Gingrich announced to the chairman of the trip, Henry Hyde, that I couldn't go because I'd been "nasty" to him. When his staff representative called to inform me I was cut, I replied, "Fine, I'm on my way to the press gallery." The staffer said, "Hold on, we'll get back to you." Surely he didn't think I'd back off my case on his misuse of Defense Department officers for a trip to Sweden. When he realized I wouldn't, he backed down quickly.

One of Newt's great political achievements was throwing the Democrats out in 1994. Among the new Republican congressmen that year were many of his own recruits.

But they rapidly became prisoners of their ideology, cloaking themselves in the sanctity of family values while their own families were coming apart at the seams. Congresswoman Enid Greene Waldholtz (Republican from Utah) was a star of this freshman class, and Newt put her on the Rules Committee—almost unheard of for a new congresswoman. (The committee is a tool of the Speaker, establishing which proposed bills will be heard. It was like handing out tickets at a bakery.) Waldholtz made her debut as Mrs. Family Values by having the first baby of the session. Newt gave her a baby shower and office space near the House floor so she could nurse. She had just held a fund-raiser for the baby's debut in Washington, everybody oohing and ahhing, when the news broke that she and her husband, Joe Waldholtz, were running a financial Ponzi game, in violation of campaign finance laws. They had a huge backlog of unpaid bills to jewelry stores and other creditors. Joe disappeared. The soap opera unraveled every day in the *Washington Post*—a massive deadbeat story. It was rather incongruous that this lawyer, counsel to one of the largest corporations in Utah, had been so duped. She claimed to have been convinced of her husband's wealth, although he never took her to his family home because he was "embarrassed" by so many servants. It became a case of: What didn't she know, and when didn't she know it?

There were other personal scandals among this family

values preaching pack, including so many infidelities and broken marriages that we joked there must be a Republican group rate from divorce lawyers, secretly calling it "Fornigate." Congressman Robert Barr (Republican from Georgia), a thrice-married Newt recruit, introduced the Defense of Marriage Act. He was worried that Hawaii might become the first state to legalize same-sex marriages. I tried to amend his bill so that marriage was defined as "monogamous" in the Judiciary Committee. Barr and his Republican colleagues voted unanimously against my amendment. I tried to toughen no-fault divorce laws when children were involved in the marriage. Once again the Republicans defeated my bill. According to Barr and his buddies, it was homosexuals and only homosexuals that were responsible for the institution of marriage crumbling. Thanks to them, for the first time in the history of the republic, we have a federal law defining marriage.

The freshmen Republicans spent the years between 1994 and 1996 pillorying all sorts of groups with their "keep hate alive" theme—homosexuals one day, welfare mothers the next, immigrants or non-English-speakers after that. Every day somebody else was causing the fall of the country. The red scare was over, so they'd have a lavender scare or a pink scare. Suddenly they were startled to find that many of their constituents thought them mean and extreme. As good politicians, they started scrambling to blur their records, trying to reinvent themselves with warm and fuzzy images.

Congressman Michael Flanagan (Republican from Illinois, now gone from the House) decided it was important to confer honorary citizenship on Mother Teresa. Congressman Henry Hyde (another Illinois Republican) used his chairmanship of the Judiciary Committee to get this bill on the House floor in record time despite an overcrowded end-of-term schedule. I knew that Flanagan wanted to be able to plaster his district with his great victory in making Mother Teresa an American, hoping that those who revered her would be so moved they would forget his rotten voting record of shooting down all the aid to the poor that Mother Teresa herself would surely have endorsed. It was a perfect political formula—politicians love to bask in the reflected glory of the person who really earned it. In my "call 'em as I see 'em" mode, I took the floor to shed a little light on this clever maneuver. I pointed out that Mother Teresa couldn't come to live in this country because the new immigration bill that Flanagan helped pass required such a foreigner to be sponsored by a relative in the United States whose income was 200 percent over the poverty line. It was wonderful to watch his reaction. Flanagan could see himself cranking out self-congratulatory letters to every Catholic parish in his district. He might be cutting aid to the poor and Head Start programs, but by God, Mother Teresa was an American.

In a way, I hated to leave Congress on a downswing, with a reactionary agenda. But I'd seen too many members stay too long. Watching the joint sessions of Congress as a child, I thought that Speaker of the House Eddie McCormack looked to be about 120. He always appeared to be falling asleep. The leader of the Senate was Carl Hayden, who looked to be 130. The two of them propped up behind the president made Congress look like it was on life support. The theme of Congress seemed to be: Elect them young, keep them alive, and move them up the escalator of power. I always promised myself I'd go out at the top of my game. I was fifty-five years old, my hair was graying, and my children were grown. I knew if I didn't leave then, I'd be a lifer, probably unemployable in the outside world. There's nothing wrong with being a lifer, but I'd never planned to be in Congress. More than two decades had gone by so fast. If ever I was to do something else, it was time.

I'd already discussed these plans with my husband, my children, my parents, who were all sad but supportive. Perhaps they also were a little bit grateful for less intrusion into their personal lives. We all know my absence from the House would mean less advocacy for the issues that mattered to us all. I called my staff together and handed them a brief declaration of my retirement, which I intended to disclose in the press gallery in one hour. I hated not giving them more lead time, but lead time equals leaks.

Announcing my retirement was a wonderfully liberating thing. I'd never been inhibited in Congress, but I was even less than my normal unrestrained self. With no political future to protect, I adapted a take-no-prisoners attitude toward colleagues who tried to steamroll women's issues.

In July of 1996, I spent one whole day waiting to present an amendment that would give the Equal Employment Opportunity Commission additional resources to manage a sexual harassment case involving Mitsubishi. The company had given a day's pay to employees from a plant in Normal, Illinois, and provided buses and meals for a "field trip" to Chicago to picket against the EEOC's intervention in this case. Congresswoman Eleanor Holmes Norton (Democrat from the District of Columbia) had chaired the EEOC during the Carter administration and had cosponsored the amendment. Finally it came up and was passed. We hadn't eaten all day and headed for the dining room. Eleanor had another amendment pending to provide funds for abortions to women in prison. Her staff was on alert to call the dining room if the bill came up. She was notified that the day's legislation was moving faster than anticipated, so she paid for her meal and headed back to the floor.

Following right behind her, I was shocked to see Congressman Chris Smith (Republican from New Jersey), who was presiding in the Speaker's chair, claiming he did not see her standing when it was time to offer her amendment. Hard to believe because she was wearing a rainbow-striped suit that stood out in the sea of dark ones. Smith is "Mr. Right to Life" in Congress. Eleanor then asked for unanimous consent to offer her amendment out of order, a courtesy extended to men all the time, no matter what the content. Over and over she requested the time, and over and over Smith objected. I was so angry at the Republican glee as they shut out Eleanor's amendment that I lost my temper, challenging them about their boorish manners and reminding them that their behavior would be captured on C-SPAN. They ended up letting Eleanor offer her amendment and voting it down.

When I announced I wasn't going to run for Congress again, I got a call from a terrific woman named Diana DeGette. She had won recognition in the Colorado state legislature with the Bubble Bill, instituting a protective zone around abortion clinics that was off-limits to disruptive right-to-lifers trying to block access to the front door. When I heard of her interest in the seat I was vacating, it seemed almost eerily perfect: She's an attorney whose husband is also a lawyer, her children are six and two (the same ages as mine when I entered Congress), and her birthday is one day before mine.

Many people asked why I didn't weigh in with an

endorsement for either Diana or Tim Sandos, another great friend who was running in the primary. Some wags even pointed out how uncharacteristically quiet I was.

I kept silent for two reasons. The first was that Denver Democrats hadn't had a choice for twenty-four years, and since it really is the voters' seat, I thought they might resent my trying to influence the outcome.

Second, there were rumblings during the primary that would have become a roar if I'd backed Diana: People were saying that women thought this was a "woman's seat." Remember, Denver is home to the Promise Keepers, so if I waded in, talk radio would have cut loose. My displeasure at the Republicans retaining control of the House was tempered by Diana's victory that November, and passing the torch to her was a joy. She does great House work, and there is a lot to do.

Leaving Congress was rather like attending my own funeral. Mostly I had to deal with paper: Every two years I'd had the right to draw a number in the lottery for offices and the opportunity to trade up. Each time I'd ask myself: Is this really a better space? Sometimes the answer was yes, sometimes no. If I was moving, we did a more thorough cleaning of the files. I'd fill cardboard boxes labeled "90th session" or "96th," put them in the hallway with my name on them, and a little truck came to shuttle them to a storage room. Suddenly I was confronted with twenty-four years of boxes. Every two years I'd also bought a leather trunk for personal souvenirs: invitations to the White House, campaign buttons, notes and photographs. I used the trunks as end tables, and when I had end-tabled the office to death, I put them in a closet. Now I had twelve trunks staring me in the face. I sent the equivalent of a huge moving van to the University of Colorado library. But I kept having farewell parties and accumulating even more stuff. (Jim would ask, "Did you take another victory lap today?") I remembered stories of Thomas Jefferson melting down the metal from all his plaques and prizes to make cups, but I was not going to open a smelter, and my kids didn't want a shrine to their mother.

Since I had moved so often, I didn't have any real sentimental attachment to the physical space I was vacating—the desk where I had kept crayons when Scott and Jamie were young had been replaced long ago. It's not as if your soul's there, like a house you've lived in. My office had never looked like anybody else's. Most congressmen have three thousand pictures of themselves on the wall. I had a Flexible Flyer and Barnum & Bailey posters—a reminder that Congress is a circus. Visiting dignitaries from Europe would sometimes say, "I think I can get an award for you," and I finally figured out that they thought I was the only person in Congress who'd never been given an award because none were on the walls.

Congress is a turnkey operation—you're constantly reminded how temporary you really are. When you leave,

you turn in your keys and the phone number gets trans-
ferred to the next person. It was difficult, during those last
weeks, knowing that my bright, talented, diligent staff was
forced to write résumés and scramble for jobs. Eighteen
people went eighteen different ways, but they all relocated
well. Some went to work in the media, some stayed in government, and some stayed in the same office, working
for the new congresswoman from Colorado's First District. Once you have politics in your bloodstream, it can
be hard to get that sense of exhilarating chaos from anything else.

On one of the few occasions I got emotional about my
leave-taking, I was in my office watching the television
that allowed me to see what was taking place on the
House floor. Ron Dellums, my ex-seatmate on the Armed
Services Committee, was recalling the time when F.
Edward Hébert was trying to intimidate the two members
at the bottom of his rung. "So the gentleman from California and the gentlewoman from Colorado had to sit in
the same chair," Ron reminisced. "We sat cheek to cheek,
hip to hip, and it took great dignity on the part of both of
us to do this. We leaned into each other, recognizing that
what was being done was the chairman's attempt to
humiliate us. It was difficult, but sitting cheek to cheek,
you learn a great deal about a person. . . . She has made
an effort to stand on the floor of this body and to challenge
this nation to commit to a rational, coherent and compas-

sionate set of human priorities." Ron and I lost a lot of our joint battles to move the world toward peace, nuclear disarmament, arms control and sanity for our military budget, but we never gave up, and I felt a real quiver in my heart about giving up now.

Not everything that was said about me in those final days was so loving and generous. I was roasted at the Hyatt Regency Washington on Capitol Hill, a humbling experience televised by C-SPAN and sponsored by the Independent Action Committee, which raises funds for independent candidates. Nora Dunn was wonderful—again—as Pat Shroeder, but the hit of the evening was Congressman John Dingell (Democrat from Michigan), who was the funniest of all. Everyone commented that Big John had a comic side they'd never seen before. (It helped, I suppose, that C-SPAN played it over and over and *over.*) One of the evening's satisfying ironies was looking into the audience and seeing Newt Gingrich's half-sister Candace among the guests.

10

Now What?

Thinking about the phenomenal democratic experiment of this country always gives me goosebumps. Our founding fathers envisioned heads of state chosen not by blood, not by elders, not by clergy, not by macho contests, not by the highest bidders. This government by, for and of the people could have only its citizens to select its leaders. Now this bold experiment seems poised on the edge of a cliff. How do we pull back?

Personal quests for power wrapped in populist or revolutionary rhetoric are ancient history. Some of our eighteenth-century ancestors distrusted the wealthy, influential colonists who challenged King George III. These wealthy leaders claimed they were rebelling so that common men would have a voice equal to theirs in affairs of state. Their idealistic proclamations were dismissed by some as another camouflaged grab for power.

When George Washington and his fellow upstarts won the revolution, the world took notice. After General Cornwallis's surrender at Yorktown, many colonists argued that Washington should be king. They said they weren't anti-monarchy, just anti-absentee monarchy. Washington refused a crown. He insisted on holding an election and letting the citizens decide who should rule. Incredible: This is what he promised to do. Is there a politician today you would offer a crown to and be confident that he or she would cling to our democratic traditions instead?

What would our forefathers think of contemporary government, with a sitting president's closest adviser caught on camera sucking a prostitute's toes? The capital seems to attract world-class hustlers and get-rich artists, trampling all over our heritage. I am not an apologist for Bill Clinton. I assign him blame for looking like a windsock on certain issues when he should have taken a firmer stand (and for ever letting Dick Morris into the Oval Office), but I think we need to pull back and look at the bigger picture. Putting aside the accusations and intimations about his private life, Clinton has done an admirable job in bringing up a daughter; he's still married and working on it. Lay that against Ronald Reagan, whose family life was a disaster, his children writing books about his neglectful parenting, posing nude in magazines or dancing in their underwear on TV. In prior times, we judged politicians by political acts. I don't understand the legal standard that says anything you've done from the time you were born, twenty-four hours a day, is subject to litigation.

As I write this, Clinton is now halfway through his second term and the sexual harassment case brought by Paula Jones is ongoing. Since she first made her charges public, she has gone through a physical transformation that would make Michael Jackson proud. But I look at things as a lawyer and a lawmaker, trying to poke through the patina of approbation that Jones is trying to muster and get to the real issue.

As one who specialized in sexual harassment legislation, I know the key to proving that charge is the fact that someone used his or her power to intimidate. I fought for the laws protecting people against such actions, and I know that this is not how we intended them to be used. If somebody invites me to his hotel room and we're two consenting adults, it's not sexual harassment if I'm dumb enough to go. The intimidation part is important, and Jones has never alleged that. If we don't insist that such a standard be kept in the law, our courtrooms will become a joke.

I continue to be astonished at the irony and hypocrisy in the Republican attacks on Bill Clinton, while letting the ethically challenged Newt Gingrich get away with murder. For two years, from 1994 to 1996, the Republicans on the House Ethics Commitee stonewalled on the charges filed against the Speaker. But in the 1996 election, the chairwoman of that committee, Nancy Johnson (Republican from Connecticut), barely held onto her seat in a very close race. Boom—Republicans got the message that voters weren't so impressed with the veil of protection around the Speaker. When Congress reconvened, the beleaguered Ethics Committee took action. Newt went from king of the hill to kickball. During his first term as Speaker, with a flick of his pinkie, his side of the aisle started doing backflips for him. In his second term, many of his Republican colleagues were plotting coups and revolts.

Cynics claim that we get the government we deserve. I say we deserve better, but we will get it only if we act. Garbage always floats to the top. That's bad news, because the top is all that most people see, and they assume it goes all the way down. But having the garbage on top is also good news, because it's easier to skim off. Contemporary congressional House work requires a broom and a skimmer.

I always felt that my job, as designed by the founding fathers, was to listen to the people, engage their minds, stir up controversy and steer clear of sanctimony. I'm proud of the fact I have never paid for a poll. The old-time view of politics held that the vox populi was important, but the person in power who has a sworn duty to lead is a little more focused than the rest of us. Now we're in a poll-and-posture mode: Whatever the poll says is what the politician's posture becomes. If the poll tells you to sit down and eat your right foot, don't ask if you get to put salt and pepper on it.

I shouldn't have to be proud of the fact that I periodically turned down free cases of Coors beer from an influential business in my state—it should be *assumed* that a politician would steer clear of those trying to curry favor. A leather-industry lobbyist once sent me a suede skirt that I loved, so I sent him a check for it. He was outraged. And a mink rancher sent me a mink coat. I told him I accepted furs only from my husband, so he sent the coat to Jim, who thought I was giving him a giant hint and bought it for me. I almost never wore it; it just wasn't me.

But such thinking makes me feel like a dinosaur. Many people believe that it's impossible for any public official to make an ethical decision, that we're all crooked and that government is a cancer. "Conservative" is pronounced with a purr, "liberal" a snarl, but the definitions of both are specious. Cynicism is the new chic ideology, approaching near epidemic proportions. The word "cynic" comes from the Greek, and democracy fell in Athens when a tidal wave of cynicism slammed down and washed it away. Many could see what was wrong but couldn't muster the will to correct it. I despair of voters who just want to vote thumbs up or thumbs down on any issue without thinking, reading or coming up with a better idea. Why do they delegate such decisions to the leaders they don't trust in the first place? Our civic responsibility is not satisfied with our thumbs. We need to put our whole selves in the game. Government is not static. It has changed many times and must change now. We should be adapting to new conditions constantly.

The honor and merit of public service established in the past will be trashed if we don't find a better way to finance campaigns. Today's methods cause people to hold their noses and turn their backs on the whole system, which virtually ensures that fat cats and their vested interests will triumph and that the price of admission to a political career is too high for all but the grandees of society or those who owe their professional lives to them. Big money tries to purchase its own agenda. Money does too much talking in Washington. Every senator, every representative, even the president awakens each morning with a number in his head that will drive the whole day. The number is the amount of money that must raised that day for his reelection. If he fails, the next day's number will be even higher.

Since it is illegal to make fund-raising calls from federal offices, our public officials spend a lot of time in their party headquarters calling the fat cats to achieve "the number." Imagine those conversations: The donors almost always have some legislative agenda they seek as a quid pro quo. When a politician reaches his number and returns to his office, a lot of time must be spent pursuing the agendas discussed with the donors. When do regular citizens weigh in? How are their voices heard? The legislative scales are totally weighted on the side of money. Money shouts its priorities. The rest of us are put on hold, growing more disenchanted by the minute. Government has become a machine that runs only when gold coins are inserted.

I had a wonderful, broad-based list of supporters from my first campaign, and I managed to keep it going by being clear how I was going to vote on issues and then actually voting that way—a refreshing notion in politics. I got some of my support out of anger at other candidates— dollar bills stuffed into envelopes with letters saying, "I'm so mad at X, Y or Z that I'm going to give you a chance." I was pleased because I always figured that anybody who bothered to give me a buck was going to vote. Lots of people feel that if they write a check as big as $25, they want to get something for it, so I was always trying to find creative, low-cost ways of fund-raising. I did pancake breakfasts and kite-flying picnics and family night at museums and summer theater subscriptions, and I spent my fortieth birthday under a halo of balloons at a performing arts center. I toyed with the idea of the world's largest pot-luck supper, but the liability was too worrisome: What if somebody got food poisoning? I did so many fund-raisers that if I made plans for dinner with my brother, he'd ask, "Do I have to pay to see you this time?"

After the 1996 election, every sentient adult knows that our campaign finance system reeks and affects everything government does, but many feel there is nothing they can do. Why can't the system be changed? Are we doomed? I think we've tackled more intractable challenges: slavery, the Depression, two world wars. We need foundations, academics and concerned citizens to convene something like a summit, drawing up core principles to measure any bill that Congress takes up under the mantle of reform. Otherwise something called "campaign finance reform" will pass. There will be all sorts of congratulatory speeches. Then several years later the loopholes will become visible, voters will feel let down again, and cynicism will grow even larger. When philosopher John Locke talked about the social compact of government, he stated that the wealthy must be held to the same levels of good conduct as the poor.

We can't survive without some government. I was thrilled to participate in ours from a front row seat. Now I want others to dig in, to run for office or at least assist those brave souls who do. Politics is not rocket science, but what else could make such a difference?

When I taught in the graduate school of government at Princeton University after I left Congress, I found to my dismay that most of my students had no intention of running for office. They wanted to work behind the scenes, to write memos and speeches for the policy-makers, rather than subjecting themselves to the ignominy of fund-raising, baring their personal lives and tax returns. They thought campaigning was too mean. These Generation X–ers, who've grown up with divorced parents, razor blades in their Halloween apples and the notion that sex can kill, wanted less risk-taking in their work.

They're not slackers. They were eager learners—I'd say, "I want you to read twenty-three books for next week," and they'd ask, "Anything else?" They're dismayed at the way Congress has abandoned our children. Why can't there be as much excitement about the growth of people as about the growth of profits? Still they don't want to wage a campaign in which having smoked a joint in college becomes a significant issue, or one that turns a murderer named Willie Horton into their running mate. I'd love to get a fund-raising letter from any of them, but I don't think I made any of them change their minds.

Princeton was like an academic theme park, with its cottages, bike paths and picturesque shops. After more than two decades of Congress's draconian schedule, university teaching was like a decompression chamber—many nights I realized I was the last person out of the building and thought I was leaving early.

But I'm still figuring out what I'm going to do for the rest of my life. Now I am president of the Association of American Publishers (AAP), the trade group for the book publishing industry. (My mother is thrilled: finally, a job she respects.) I love this work because books are brain food. If every American would purchase the equivalent of his weight in books each year, this country would be a different place.

Protecting intellectual property is my main focus at AAP. Technology has made it so easy to copy anything you create, people forget it is not one whit easier to generate an idea than it was a millennium ago. American creativity has fueled our economy and sustained our middle class. While it seems that anything we manufacture can be produced more cheaply offshore somewhere, that's not true of the products of our creativity.

There is now a great faux-populist movement that says intellectual property should be free to anyone who wants it. The argument goes that people write songs and books for people to hear and read, so let them. But most of these writers still like to eat and pay the rent.

When I'm not defending intellectual property, I'm trying to figure out how to alert our society to the crucial importances of reading aloud to children every day. Most people think it's "nice" to do, but the research is clear: Reading aloud to children is as necessary to their development and to our future as proper nutrition. So we're looking at ways to give books the razzle-dazzle other media have. Reading may not have the flash of, say, MTV, but it's clearly the on ramp to the twenty-first century.

I've also been working with Pam Solo, a dear friend who ran my presidential campaign. She now heads the Institute for a Civil Society, a think tank with a $35 million endowment from a New England family that wants to remain anonymous. "Civility" is a new buzzword in Washington, but it's often just an excuse for not debating critical issues, for fear of offending someone. Vigorous debate without personal attack is our heritage. A "civil society" cannot be muzzled—we must debate critical issues. Our communities must reweave the torn fabric of society, recreating the infrastructure and connectedness to each other that we are rapidly losing. Americans with money are bailing out of our civil society at a frantic pace: fleeing to gated communities, to private schools, even to a separate legal system for the wealthy. I fear we are gating our hearts in the process.

The Institute for a Civil Society is trying to rebuild community confidence. As director of a program called "New Solutions for a New Century," I have a five-year mission to find people who are rebuilding their communities and become partners with them. We'd like to create a "good news bulletin board," posting ideas that have been tested and found successful, so that other communities don't have to start from square one. As one of our first projects, we have partnered with the Interamerican Development Bank on a conference about violence in the home. The bank stated clearly domestic violence is an economic issue and health issue. In some parts of Latin America, there are no divorce laws, and if a woman who has been battered gets an annulment, it means she was never married. That could be economically devastating to her. We had talk radio shows come into the bank and broadcast throughout the conference. We reached more than twenty million people. We've met with people in Brazil to discuss the idea of *telenovellas* or soap operas whose heroes are women who break the cycle of domestic violence. From the bank on down, the institute is trying to find innovative ways to crack the cultural acceptance of domestic violence.

I can't imagine *not* working on behalf of causes that will improve the family, the nation, the world, the planet. In my dotage, rocking on my porch, I will probably be faxing or e-mailing or communicating by whatever twenty-first century method I cannot even fathom about social wrongs that need to be righted.

Go ahead and say it: I am a bleeding-heart liberal. Think about how much better society would be if each of us felt a special calling in life, something that stirred our passions and empowered our efforts, and we took action on those passions, whether they be literacy or Alzheimer's or whales. My passions have always been stirred by the dilemmas of children, the families, and how this diverse nation makes good on its promise of equality.

As a young wife and mother, I discovered the frustration of housework. No matter how much I dusted, vacuumed, changed bed linens and washed dishes, I had to do it again and again. Congressional House work was just the same, with interminable battles and infinite targets.

Our work as citizens is a lot like housework: It never ends. We can either wring our hands in despair or use them to roll up our shirtsleeves and try to find new ways to make a difference.

I have no time for a lot of wringing but a lot of time for shirtsleeve-rolling. It can get lonely. Consider this a postcard from the front. Wish you were here. Roll 'em up!

Postscript

Whoever thought the first person to be "impeached" by Monica Lewinsky would be Newt Gingrich? Last year, as I closed out the hardcover edition of this book, the Krakatoa of all political eruptions hit the White House. The news was all Monica all the time. Every American heard Monica's name but no one heard her voice for months.

Then came the November 3, 1998, election. Pundits proclaimed for weeks there would be a landslide victory for the Republicans. If the president's sex scandal with a White House intern didn't send droves of mad Americans to the polls, what would? Well, we don't know what would because instead of a Republican landslide there were Republican losses. Democrats who were supposed to be too demoralized to vote, weren't. Minnesota votes exhibited a playfulness that surprised the nation. They elected a governor on Perot's reform ticket known as Jesse "The Body" Ventura. Was the heart of the nation telling us something?

For a while it looked like the president had escaped impeachment and a censure would be negotiated. Then the news became all impeachment all the time—with a brief break for bombing Iraq. With the holidays pressing down, the president ordered the bombing of Saddam Hussein and the House of Representatives voted impeachment. So what happens in 1999?

The Senate will try the case made by the House against the president. The sight of one hundred senators in their seats unable to ask questions is a vision no one ever thought they would see, but impeachment rules will make that a reality. Few currently think the Senate will have the necessary two-thirds votes to impeach, and the president says he will not resign. But who knows? I have sent my crystal ball out to be repaired.

Sadly, for all the changes this year, one thing remains the same. In the House both parties rejected the congresswomen who ran for leadership positions. So the House will enter the twenty-first century as it did the twentieth, with no women in positions of leadership. At least in the twenty-first century women are voting and members. Sigh . . . I'd like more progress.

What does all this mean? For those who read this book's early edition and said, "Nice view of the past but things will never be that fluid again," I think this year proved them wrong. Our political system is up for grabs. All of us must encourage young people to engage in the system—otherwise cynicism will drown our nation's future. If you don't think things can change, look at

November 3, 1998. The cement cracked around the feet of our most powerful and Newt Gingrich was gone in days. It's a system that works if the citizens do. Roll up your sleeves and continue the housekeeping tradition.